"Get Off Your Donkey! is a challenge ȶ̣ȶ ̣ᴀ̣ɪ̣ ̣⸝̣
live their lives like Jesus—to love and serve others. In the process, we help ourselves. What a fabulous message! What a wonderful book! Thank you, Reggie."

—**Ken Blanchard**, coauthor, *The One Minute Manager* and *Lead Like Jesus*

"Jesus calls us to be neighbors to those around us, and Reggie McNeal spells out what that means in contemporary social settings. In this inspiring book, we have biblically based courses of action and illustrations that are invaluable for those who want to live out Jesus's imperative to love our neighbors as ourselves."

—**Tony Campolo**, emeritus professor of sociology, Eastern University

"Reggie's new book vacillates from very good to fabulously good. In fact, this book is so good I don't want to talk about it here. Read it, and then we'll talk."

—**Leonard Sweet**, bestselling author; professor, Drew University and George Fox University; chief contributor to www.sermons.com

"If you've ever wondered what God wants you to do with your life, Reggie McNeal has written a book that will show you exactly how and where to get started. As always, he writes in a way that touches minds, hearts, and funny bones. And as you might guess from the title, it all starts with the decision to get off your . . . well, donkey."

—**Larry Osborne**, author and pastor, North Coast Church, Vista, California

"In *Get Off Your Donkey!* Reggie McNeal brilliantly examines one of the elements central to well-being: well-doing.

His book will change how you think about the role of religion and spirituality in leading a thriving (and well-doing) life."

—James K. Harter, chief scientist, The Gallup Organization; *New York Times* bestselling author

"For everyone who wants to make a difference, whether it be in your community, school, or social setting, this is a must-read."

—Eric Cooper, president and CEO, San Antonio Food Bank

"Transformation happens when we respond to God's invitation to meet someone else's need. Not only does it help our neighbor, it touches a deep need in our own lives that results in real joy. Reggie once again has given us a timely book that will stir hearts. His words deliver provocative truth coupled with punching humor. Don't stop reading until you clearly hear God's call to action."

—Tom Wilson, CEO, Echo Clinics

"Reggie McNeal unravels the parable of the Good Samaritan. Contrasting serving God at church with serving our neighbor, he artfully offers practical advice on how to show God's love to our neighbor. Truly inspiring, *Get Off Your Donkey!* is a must-read for church leaders."

—John Jenkins, senior pastor, First Baptist Church of Glenarden, Upper Marlboro, Maryland

GET OFF YOUR DONKEY!

GET OFF YOUR DONKEY!

Help Somebody and Help Yourself

REGGIE McNEAL

BakerBooks

a division of Baker Publishing Group
Grand Rapids, Michigan

Published by Baker Books
a division of Baker Publishing Group
P.O. Box 6287, Grand Rapids, MI 49516-6287
www.bakerbooks.com

Printed in the United States of America

Library of Congress Cataloging-in-Publication Data
McNeal, Reggie.
    Get off your donkey! : help somebody and help yourself / Reggie McNeal.
       p.   cm.
    Includes bibliographical references.
    ISBN 978-0-8010-1497-0 (pbk.)
    1. Christian life. 2. Service (Theology) I.Title.
BV4509.5.M363 2013
248.4—dc23   2012035476

14   15   16   17   18   19   7   6   5   4   3

In keeping with biblical principles of creation stewardship, Baker Publishing Group advocates the responsible use of our natural resources. As a member of the Green Press Initiative, our company uses recycled paper when possible. The text paper of this book is composed in part of post-consumer waste.

To Henry, Melanie, Chandler, Hannah,
Mark, Pam, Leah, and Cathy

CONTENTS

ACKNOWLEDGMENTS

I don't know how it is for other authors, but I always find the acknowledgments section one of the most difficult sections of the book to write. Not because I am not grateful or because no one comes to mind as a major contributor to the project. Just the opposite is true. So *many* people come to mind, it's hard to settle on just whom to single out.

After all, where does a book idea come from? I can claim and honestly think that I came up with it all by myself. But how many conversations with how many people did it take to form a coherent "plot" for the book's content? Countless. And they all mattered, though I can't pick out one that by itself gave birth or shape to the book (just like I can't remember what I've had for dinner every night of my life, but I am alive and portly to prove that I showed up to eat routinely—and enthusiastically).

Let me just acknowledge all those who contributed to the content of this book as the unnamed heroes—the people I have met and continue to meet who inspire me with their service to their neighbors and their communities. They refuse to accept the status quo, choosing instead to believe and to deliver help and hope. They show us all the way.

While the lives and examples of these unnamed heroes provide the soul and seedling of this book, there are some people I can name who have provided their expertise to bring this volume to market.

Mark Sweeney not only believed in this project, he sold it! As my literary agent, he delivers the right combination of honest feedback and encouragement to keep me going. He is the kind of friend everyone needs working for them!

The crew at Baker Books deserves a huge shout-out for taking a risk on this project. In a culture of such PC awareness, where everyone's looking to be offended at something in some way, they decided to put out a tongue-in-cheek title for a very serious subject they care about deeply. Kudos to them! Chad Allen, the main project leader, was the first to put his donkey on the line for this book. Without his endorsement and sponsorship, I wouldn't have gotten to know Mike Cook, Ruth Anderson, Anna Scianna, or Jessica English, or experience their enthusiastic professionalism. Thanks, gang—you can all go home now!

No man could have a better personal cheerleader and consultant on everything than I have had for over three decades now—all wrapped up in one person who also happens to be my wife. Thanks, Cate! You make the trip so much fun.

Lastly, I am grateful to all those in our communities who are working this moment to turn the tide. I hope others will join you soon!

INTRODUCTION

I was speaking to a group of church and community leaders about Jesus's parable of the Good Samaritan. I pointed out that loving our neighbors is apparently a big deal to Jesus, since in the story the command to serve others ranks right up there with the instruction to love God. I commented that with his tale, Jesus gigged religious people for missing the point. The hero of the story—with suspect spiritual credentials for the church crowd—is the only person who reflects God's heart for the person in need.

"The moral of the story," I quipped, "is that you have to get off your donkey to help somebody." The few people who giggled in the audience made me realize what I had just said.

A few months later I was asked to speak at a denomination's annual tribal gathering. I decided again to speak on the Good Samaritan story, and remembering the earlier episode, I responded with a tongue-in-cheek reply to an email requesting the title of my talk. "Get Off Your Donkey!" was what I sent in, thinking I would get some sort of fun exchange going. I never heard back. Weeks later I learned that the program had been printed with the title, the production team apparently oblivious to the joke. Maybe if I had substituted King James language for *donkey*, they would have gotten it! The import of the title was not lost on the crowd, however. We had great fun together as I prodded them to take action.

As a conference speaker, I travel a lot. "What kind of business are you in?" is a frequent question I get asked by airplane seatmates strapped alongside me for the ride.

"I work in leadership development," I usually say. That response typically generates a follow-up question.

"Who do you work with?" they ask with interest.

"Mostly with church leaders," I reply.

"Uh-huh," they typically respond, returning to their smartphones or laptops, their enthusiasm level noticeably dampened.

Then I say, "I'm trying to help them get out of the church business and into the people business." This comment generally provokes interest and sometimes fascinating conversation. In case they don't know Jesus, even if they attend church, I want them to know that he actually *is* in the people business.

What does this discussion of airplane chatter have to do with getting off donkeys? Simply this: I don't know what business you are in (education, the social sector, for-profit enterprise, health care), but ultimately you want to be in the people business. Why do I say this? Because helping people is the best part of life! If you don't discover this truth and act on it, not only will your neighbors' needs go unmet, but *you* will never be whole. And if that's not reason enough to motivate you to love your neighbor, know that the further consequences of your inaction will guarantee a diminished future not just for them and for you but also for our whole society.

The toll of institutional failure in American government, education, finances, and health care—and yes, even the church—is resulting in catastrophic loss for millions. The cost is not only devastating in individual terms; the future of our country is at stake. The Great Recession and its aftermath have raised a specter of a "new normal" that signals the possible twilight of American civilization. The creativity and resiliency that have been hallmarks of our culture are eroding away to a mind-set colored by a lack of confidence and pessimism that is sapping our resolve and threatening our capacity to meet these challenges.

This does not have to be twilight in America. Not if we take personal responsibility for loving our neighbors as ourselves, for meeting needs as we are able. It is time for all of us to get up off whatever we're sitting on and help somebody!

This book is a call to action. Maybe you can't change the world, but you can change your street. You may not be able to change your community's overall graduation rates, but you can mentor a kid out of becoming a high school dropout. Wiping out hunger might be too daunting a task, but packing food into schoolkids' backpacks so they can eat over the weekend is doable. If enough of us get off our donkeys—determined to be a part of the solution to address others' problems—we can arrest the downhill slide for many people, maybe even our communities and our country.

> *It is time for all of us to get up off whatever we're sitting on and help somebody!*

I am writing this book for anyone and everyone who wants to stem the darkness, but I anticipate that a bunch of readers will be church people. Here's a heads-up for you. I take square aim at an unbiblical churchianity that has resulted in a church-centric religion that fails to reflect the heart of God for people. Not only have our communities been underserved with this misplaced emphasis, but those practicing churchianity report anemic spiritual lives for all their institutional religious involvement. The result has been a church that passes by on the other side of the road when we should be the ones showing the way.

15

Rising poverty is not solely the result of failed government programs; it is happening also because the church has refused to be the church Jesus imagined. If kids are not graduating from our schools because they lack the ability to read, it is not just a failure of our educational system; it is also a failure of the church, because our congregations are full of people who can read! The examples of social ills could go on and on, and I would offer in each case the same challenge to the church.

The church should be calling the party in every community—a party convened to solve our biggest problems. I am not talking about a church takeover of other society sectors. I am calling on the church to offer its best resources to the community and to galvanize the efforts of the community to tackle the issues that threaten the welfare of its people. This kind of service leadership provides the only way for the church to regain favor in America. The leadership by pontification and moral snootiness of the last few decades resembles the Pharisee religion that Jesus detested. We might as well try it his way!

Unfortunately, I run into people every week who are unwittingly (and sometimes wittingly) caught in the web of religious activity as a sad substitution for spiritual vitality. The good news is that when I call them back to what it really means to be God's people, it is like I am announcing a jail-break. People are ready! Ready to quit meaningless institutional religion. Ready to make a difference in other people's lives. Ready to live for something that is worth living for. Ready to get off their donkeys and help somebody.

There is also a second theme in this book. It is the connection between serving others and the improved quality of our own life. In the process of helping others, we help ourselves. I'm not just inviting you to a life *of* service; I maintain that you'll get a life *through* service. I am not suggesting that we love our neighbors for selfish reasons. But service to others carries its own life-enriching rewards for the ones doing the serving.

The best strategy for experiencing the abundant life that Jesus talked about is through loving our neighbors. Taking this approach to life guarantees our own self-development. On the flip side, our self-development increases our capacity for service to others. This is a wonderful synergy that we will explore for most of these pages.

Let me say who I hope will read this book and take its message to the streets. First, I want to help followers of Jesus who are ready to *be* church right where they are already deployed seven days a week, in their neighborhoods, workplaces, schools, homes—wherever they live their lives. If this is you, I'd like to help you recalibrate your spiritual efforts for greater life rewards—in others and in you. I want to give you permission and validation for expressing your faith in everyday life rhythms, not just involvement in institutional churchianity.

> I'm not just inviting you to a life *of* service; I maintain that you'll get a life **through** service.

The second group I have in mind is the growing number of courageous church leaders who are not just willing but determined to change their ministry scorecards, both personally for themselves and corporately for those in their leadership constellation of influence. Acutely aware of the impotence of the institutional church to deliver spiritual growth for its participants, they are even more horrified by its failure to demonstrate the character of Jesus to the world. These leaders are making radical shifts in how they live and lead. They encourage me to believe that the church's best days are ahead as followers of Jesus demonstrate incarnational love. I want to give these leaders a resource they can use with those they lead that will help create greater kingdom engagement.

The third readership hopefully includes people who do not consider themselves followers of Jesus but who want to contribute to other people's needs and to their communities. In the parable of the Good Samaritan, the hero fits into this category. Everyone who does good has joined God's kingdom agenda, because the kingdom is about people and about life. I want to celebrate their efforts. I want to escalate the altruism of people who instinctively know that their better self is one given to helping others. This book hopefully can create synergy between and among all Americans who want their lives to make a positive contribution to their communities and to the people around them.

I hope that this book prompts a conversation within you as well. Throughout the discussion, I will ask you some questions designed to help you capture your thoughts along the way. I've included some space for reflection where you can write down your responses to the questions. (If you're reading this on an e-reading device, it might be worthwhile to pick up a journal or notebook so you'll be able to record your reflections and keep them in place for reference later.) Not every question will resonate with you, but hopefully enough of them will prompt a response. Eventually you might simply flip back through your answers and thoughts for insights into what you want to do with the rest of your life.

A lot is at stake. I am writing to move you to action. We all have to get off our donkeys. Nothing less than the fate of America, your community, your neighbor—even you—depends on it!

1

A CHOICE TO MAKE

I blew it. And I knew it. I had missed the chance. All the way home on the plane I rehearsed the missed opportunity. Earlier that day thousands of church leaders attending a leadership conference had heard me passionately address the need for the church to reimagine itself and its mission in the world. I had gotten carried away, talked too long about unimportant things, and found myself suddenly out of time. I concluded with a lame ending that failed to do the one thing I had intended to do: call those leaders to action!

Instead, I settled for persuasion, for an interesting presentation. But no call to *do* something.

Late that night, finally alone with God back home, I apologized to him. I told him if he would give me another chance, I would not fail to challenge people to step up and step out to serve those in the community around them.

This book is part of the way I am following through with my apologetic commitment to God. I don't think you will miss the point I'm making. It's time for you and me to *do* something!

America is struggling for its life. Your gut is telling you that the future outcome of our country is being decided right now. You are right! Either we are headed into a death spiral, or we are going to find our way forward and out of this mess. The outcome is up to you. A clear choice is involved. You must decide whether or not you will improve the lives of people around you.

Unfortunately, a bunch of people are giving in to despair, believing that our future inevitably is going to be worse than our past, that our best days are behind us, that we've somehow lost something we can't recover and we are entering the twilight of America. This attitude isn't going to get us anywhere except somewhere we don't want to go!

Assigning blame will not cure the situation either. Without question, there is plenty of it to go around. And people should be held accountable for their actions. Our institutions have failed us. Our political system has become too political. The financial system is bankrupt. Health care is caught somewhere between the emergency room and hospice care. Our educational system has a failing grade heading into finals. We trusted these institutions to deliver, but they have dropped the ball and seem incapable of recovering their own fumble.

Maybe we need to be reminded that our institutions do not hold exclusive rights to the future of our country. You and I have a lot to say about it.

Recently in my local paper, there was a story commemorating the death of a woman who was known as the "dime lady." Some years ago she began collecting dimes to give to the local food bank. Her church joined in by setting up receptacles where people could toss in their loose change. Over time, the woman gave tens of thousands of dollars to fight hunger in our region, all from a simple behavior she adopted. Even though the woman had no personal wealth to speak of, she was able to make a big contribution to the cause that had captured her heart. The "dime lady" refused to accept an unacceptable situation or succumb to an "I can't do anything about it" mentality.

Each of us holds the same key that unlocks a better future—for us and for our communities and nation. It is the choice to do good to others, especially to those in need around us. If enough of us exercise the option to use this key, to insert it into the door to the future, we can unlock a better future than the one that looms ahead of us now. We can arrest the downward slide of our country.

A Story-in-the-Book Beginning

The idea for this book's title came to me as I reflected on one of Jesus's best-known stories. He told the story to answer a question raised by a religious expert. The questioner wanted to know how to secure life in the hereafter. Jesus's response moved the focus into the here and now.

Here is the entire exchange, including the background conversation. We know this episode by its central story: we call it the parable of the Good Samaritan.

> On one occasion an expert in the law stood up to test Jesus. "Teacher," he asked, "what must I do to inherit eternal life?"
>
> "What is written in the Law?" he replied. "How do you read it?"
>
> He answered, "'Love the Lord your God with all your heart and with all your soul and with all your strength and with all your mind'; and, 'Love your neighbor as yourself.'"
>
> "You have answered correctly," Jesus replied. "Do this and you will live."
>
> But he wanted to justify himself, so he asked Jesus, "And who is my neighbor?"
>
> In reply Jesus said: "A man was going down from Jerusalem to Jericho, when he was attacked by robbers. They stripped him of his clothes, beat him and went away, leaving him half

dead. A priest happened to be going down the same road, and when he saw the man, he passed by on the other side. So too, a Levite, when he came to the place and saw him, passed by on the other side. But a Samaritan, as he traveled, came where the man was; and when he saw him, he took pity on him. He went to him and bandaged his wounds, pouring on oil and wine. Then he put the man on his own donkey, brought him to an inn and took care of him. The next day he took out two denarii and gave them to the innkeeper. 'Look after him,' he said, 'and when I return, I will reimburse you for any extra expense you may have.'

"Which of these three do you think was a neighbor to the man who fell into the hands of robbers?"

The expert in the law replied, "The one who had mercy on him."

Jesus told him, "Go and do likewise." (Luke 10:25–37)

Two things in this story jump out at me. First, the Samaritan had to get off his donkey to help the victim. As opposed to others in the tale, he stopped what he was doing to become engaged with the plight of the robbed-and-beat-up person. He then gave up his own seat to the injured man, letting him ride on his donkey to an inn where he could recuperate.

Second, Jesus ended the episode with a clear instruction: "Go and *do* likewise" (emphasis added). He didn't say "go and *agree with my teaching* likewise" or "go and *debate your own course of action* likewise" or "go and *lament the course of things* likewise." He said "go and *do* likewise."

While there are lots of applications for us from this well-known story (which we will get to shortly), the bottom line is you and I have to get off our donkeys if we want to make a difference. Now!

As I have said, there is no shortage of voices telling us how bad things are. A friend of mine emailed me recently to say that after listening to a news story on the economic crisis in

Europe (it was Greek week), he was "scared to death about what's going to happen to me, my children, America, the whole dang world." He is not alone. A culture of 24-7 news coverage of wars, weather calamities, stock market fluctuations, and artificial reality shows can't help but instill in its viewers and listeners constant and heightened anxiety.

During a recent morning commute, I counted the number of "crises" the radio served up to me. The drive took only twenty minutes. Yet the list of impending disasters that were brought to my attention numbered over a dozen in that small amount of time. One thirty-second blurb urged me to buy a precious metal as a hedge against economic meltdown. Another warned me of the dangers of cell phone radiation. Still another suggested that while I was driving in my car, the phone lines were being cut to my alarm system at home. Global warming got in there somehow, along with hair loss. I was depressed by 7:47 a.m., and the day hadn't even served up its real challenges!

> We can't afford to let all this negative vibe paralyze us into inactivity while people are bleeding out all around us.

I am not writing this book to join the chorus of conspirators and anxiety peddlers. What I *am* attempting to convey is that we can't afford to let this negative vibe paralyze us into inactivity while people are bleeding out all around us.

I'm weary of listening to all the angry people on radio and cable shows telling me I need to be fed up with this or that. *They* are what I'm fed up with. I'm mad as heck with people telling me they are mad as hell! All that negative energy is siphoning off the precious energy we need to help somebody.

There is hope! But that hope is not just going to materialize before you. You are going to have to work for it. As you and I and millions of others get off our donkeys, we can deal with our most vexing problems and the people chewed up by them. As we deliver help and hope to those who need it, we will gain renewed conviction that we can be part of making our communities and our country better.

I am no Pollyanna. There is plenty in me that likes to point out what's wrong with things (after all, I'm a consultant!). I am under no illusions that we will build a utopia or eradicate all the negative forces in our country. It's just that I'm not going down without a fight! I want to push back darkness where I can. I don't accept as inevitable our national decline. Besides, when my "better angels" come out to play and I actually do something to improve other people's lives, I find energy and meaning. I become more of the person that I too want to be.

Lessons from the Good Samaritan Story

Some themes emerge in the story lines of the parable of the Good Samaritan that we can apply to our current day.

- *People all around us are half dead or down-and-out. All kinds of thieves have bushwhacked our fellow citizens.* Institutional poverty, loss of jobs, health crises, emotional hardships, and usually a combination of the above afflict many people in our communities. When our fellow citizens suffer, so does our country. Every person who goes to bed hungry at night gnaws at our nation's well-being. Every job lost in our community subtracts from our bottom lines. Every kid not learning to read signals a failing grade for us. We are all in this boat together. Need calls for a neighbor!
- *We can choose to pass by on the other side of the road.* Two out of three people in the story did not stop to help the victim. Lots of forces conspire to favor this option. I

24

will identify these forces in the next chapter—so we can kick them to the curb! You and I have no excuse not to be helpful. We've got to dismount.

- *We have to be more than empathetic. We have to actually be helpful!* The Good Samaritan addressed the man's wounds with wine and oil. People in the first century had no germ theory; they just knew that wine and oil helped to fight infection and stimulate healing. Our helper in the story did everything he knew to do. Similarly, we all have competencies and skills to offer those in need. We have to pony up. I will help you identify where you can be helpful and how, just what it is you bring to the table, and how you can further develop your contribution.

> Jesus made it plain that loving our neighbor means engaging with people who need our help.

- *Jesus expanded the idea of "neighbor" from the people next door or down the street to a broader category: people in need.* These might be people who are or who are not like us, people we don't normally hang out with, or people who don't live near us. Referring to the cast of characters in his tale, Jesus asked, "Which of these three do you think was a neighbor to the man who fell into the hands of robbers?" The answer exploded the idea of neighbor as a relationship defined by a street address. The helper and the helpee in the story probably didn't even live in the same town. Their social circle was not the same for sure. Jesus made it plain that loving our neighbor means engaging with people who need our help. We pass these people every day—not just people broken down on the road (although they certainly qualify), but all those who have been beaten and robbed. The thieves can be drugs, illiteracy, joblessness, crime—whatever robs people of life.

- *The helper in the story knew when he needed to partner with others for a full recovery.* He tag-teamed with the innkeeper to ensure the injured man would get what he needed. Sometimes you may choose to help someone as a solo effort. Maybe you don't want anyone else to know about what you're doing. Or maybe you have all that's needed for a solution to a problem. However, many of the issues that plague our neighbors and communities are going to require a bunch of us to pitch in together. You may find yourself forming collaborative partnerships with others in your community to work for the alleviation of certain problems. And some of you already prefer to work with people around you, so your natural inclination will be to involve others in what you do.

Reflection: Do any of these "lessons" give you any new insights or inspire other thoughts about serving or being a good neighbor?

Kingdom Come

As I have mentioned, the Good Samaritan story is an example of Jesus's focus on life in the here and now as the arena for demonstrating the kingdom of God. Jesus was obsessed with the kingdom. It was not just an idea to hope for; it was his operating reality, his message, his very mission. All four Gospels make this plain.

Jesus went through all the towns and villages, teaching in their synagogues, preaching the good news of the kingdom and healing every disease and sickness. (Matt. 9:35, emphasis added)

Jesus went into Galilee, proclaiming the good news of God. "The time has come," he said. "The kingdom of God has come near." (Mark 1:14–15, emphasis added)

He said, "I must proclaim the good news of the kingdom of God to the other towns also, because that is why I was sent." (Luke 4:43, emphasis added)

"You are a king, then!" said Pilate.
Jesus answered, "You say that I am a king." (John 18:37, emphasis added)

You can find dozens of other references to the kingdom of heaven or kingdom of God connected to Jesus throughout the Gospels. Also, the book of Acts, narrating the post-resurrection, preascension chapter of Jesus's time on earth with his disciples, says that he "spoke about the kingdom of God" (Acts 1:3). He apparently wanted to leave his followers thinking about what he had encouraged them to do earlier when he said, "Seek first his [God's] kingdom" (Matt. 6:33).

During Jesus's public ministry, his teaching on the kingdom of *heaven* was accompanied by *earthly* miracles of healing. This created quite a stir about him, landing him on the front page in every town he visited. While Jesus admitted his kingdom was not of this world, he taught his disciples to pray for this heavenly kingdom to come to earth (see Matt. 6:10). It is supposed to show up here, now, every day, in tangible ways.

Jesus chose to explain himself to his own hometown crowd in kingdom terms. He characterized his mission like this, borrowing the language of Isaiah 61:1–2: "The Spirit of the Lord is on me, because he has anointed me to proclaim good news to the poor. He has sent me to proclaim freedom for the prisoners and recovery of sight for the blind, to set the oppressed free, to proclaim the year of the Lord's favor" (Luke 4:18–19). Jesus obviously viewed his kingdom assignment in a concrete, demonstrable way.

John the Baptist sent his disciples to Jesus with the question, "Are you the one?" (Matt. 11:3). Jesus's reply pointed John to the kingdom: "Go back and report to John what you hear and see: The blind receive sight, the lame walk, those who have leprosy are cleansed, the deaf hear, the dead are raised, and the good news is proclaimed to the poor" (Matt. 11:4–5). Again, these were the hoped-for results and signs of the outbreak of the kingdom of God. Maybe this kingdom perspective—grounded in heaven but showing up on earth—is why Jesus said, "I have come that they may have life, and have it *to the full*" (John 10:10, emphasis added). What if Jesus was telling the truth? What if he really intended to make life good for people? And what if he intends to do so through us?

> What if Jesus was telling the truth? What if he really intended to make life good for people? And what if he intends to do so through us?

When Jesus talked about loving our neighbors in terms of alleviating pain and suffering, he was reflecting his kingdom perspective. What that means to you and me is that when we do good to others, we are in cahoots with God!

The truth is that anyone working to better people's lives is reflecting the heart of God. Jesus illustrated this point in the story by making the hero a Samaritan. For his listeners, that choice had to be quite a stretch. Samaritans were suspect in their religion, actually considered outsiders in faith terms. They were viewed as ethnically inferior by the pure-blooded Jews, since they were the offspring of marriages between Jews and other people groups. In other words, religious and racial prejudices colored every aspect of Jewish-Samaritan relationships. So when Jesus made a Samaritan the hero of a story, it really challenged his audience.

But this approach was not uncharacteristic of Jesus. He had a habit of yukking it up with outsiders, the marginalized, the outcasts. He would hang out with just anybody, it seemed, from lowlife traitors like Zacchaeus to social and religious snobs like Simon the Pharisee, but he seemed to favor more common people. He chose fishermen and women to be in his circle, a very unusual choice of followers. The religious elite constantly pointed out his choice of associates as a major reason they didn't think he was qualified to be a bona fide spiritual leader. Even Jesus's hometown synagogue message managed to tick off the audience, because all the illustrations Jesus used of God's miraculous interventions focused on episodes involving foreigners, even enemies of Israel. Jesus made it plain to the people of Nazareth that God's work extended to groups and individuals not considered to be God's people. (You can read the whole story of that experience in Luke 4:16–30.)

What all this means is that a bunch of people on the planet are engaged in kingdom activity—even if they are unaware of it. It also means that those of us who claim to be followers of Jesus reflect his heart only if we are joining in these kingdom efforts. We might be involved in a bunch of religious church activity (like the priest and Levite in the parable), but that doesn't automatically connect us with God's agenda. The first hearers of Jesus's story didn't miss this. Jesus went out of his way to make the point. Church people in the story didn't come out looking too good, but a Samaritan did.

Reflection: Where and how do you see the kingdom of God breaking in around you?

_____

_____

_____

Church and Kingdom

As I said in the introduction to this book, I am not writing exclusively to church people. However, I anticipate that a number of Jesus-followers will read this and that many of them are part of a local congregation. So, since I have introduced the kingdom of God into this discussion, I think I need to make a few comments about the relationship between the church and the kingdom. My reason for doing so is to make the case that helping others is what aligns us with God's primary mission on earth. Unfortunately for many, this truth has been obscured by an improper understanding of where and how the church fits into God's mission and the kingdom. I want to clear up some confusion here in order to both give permission to and challenge church people to come out and play!

Jesus made it plain that God's primary mission has to do with building and extending his kingdom. The church is *not* his major agenda. Nor does the church own the kingdom or the mission of God. God's mission involves the redemptive restoration of everything that sin has tarnished and broken.

This mission predates the church. God's mission was under way in the Garden of Eden, centuries before he created a special people in his covenant with Abraham. And the mission will outlast the church. In the book of Revelation, there is no church in the eternal city. So we begin and end the Bible with no church. The church has a creation point, and it has a terminus. The kingdom, on the other hand, is forever—a truth rehearsed every time we utter the Lord's Prayer! The church is not our ultimate destination; the kingdom is.

I am hoping to get God's people more engaged in kingdom affairs and less preoccupied with church stuff. In fact, I think the scorecard of the church needs to be recalibrated to focus more on helping people. This change will require the reallocation of church resources (including the time, talent, and treasure of church people) to support a more kingdom-centric and less church-centric approach to expressing what it means to be the people of God.

By *church-centric*, I mean an agenda that focuses and funnels our resources into building the church, with the idea that advancing the church is the primary expression of the kingdom. The assumption that goes along with this perspective is that if we build great churches, we automatically will see better communities. This line of thinking has led to an increasingly self-absorbed and consumerist church culture that has become more *of* the world and less *in* it—the exact opposite of the sentiments Jesus expressed in his prayer in Gethsemane on the eve of his crucifixion (see John 17). When it is consumed with its own programming and projects, the church has forsaken its appropriate place in the kingdom.

I don't make these statements because I don't like the church. Just the opposite. I love the church! I just want it to come to its biblical senses, to its real identity and role. When the people of God recover what it really means to be the people of God, we will have a chance at changing the current negative narrative for both the church and our country.

The good news is that increasingly, church leaders and congregations are embracing a more kingdom-centric engagement with their communities. Just today a book arrived in the mail detailing one congregation's involvement with everything from street ministry to the homeless to providing medical care through free clinics to mobile food delivery. This array of services is becoming more typical in every city across all denominations. It is a renewal of the church through ministry *outside* the church. All of these initiatives are signs that the church is getting the point of what it means to *be* the church.

God created the church to be a people partnering with him in his redemptive mission in the world. Let's break that down.

- *The people of God.* Genesis 12:1–2 records God's creation of a special people who are to live in covenant with him. The call of Abraham begins a metanarrative that runs throughout the whole Bible. The church entered this story when believers were made heirs to the covenant through the sacrificial work of Jesus on the cross. This covenantal relationship was memorialized by Jesus at the Last Supper and is celebrated every time the Lord's Supper is observed by his followers. The church is a people; it's not an institution or organization, though it has institutional and organizational features and functions. Said another way, the church is a *who*, not a *what*. It is a relationship between God and a chosen people.

> God created the church to be a people partnering with him in his redemptive mission in the world.

- *Partnering with God.* The point of being chosen is not so we can focus on being chosen. Belonging to him is not the point of being chosen either. During the Exodus experience, God reminded Israel of the point of being chosen: "Now if you obey me fully and keep my covenant, then out of all nations you will be my treasured possession. Although the *whole earth* is mine, you will be for me a kingdom of priests and a holy nation" (Exod. 19:5–6, emphasis added). The specialness of being the people of God resides solely in the covenant: "If you obey me fully and keep my covenant" (v. 5). The covenant means we have a role to perform, a special assignment. This assignment is to partner with God in his mission. That's the point of what it means to be chosen.

When God called Abraham, his mission had been under way for centuries. But God gave Abraham a special assignment. This assignment, now belonging to the church, spells out our specific partnership role in the mission. Our job is to bless the world. When we do, people are turned toward God. Being the people of God means being people of blessing. No one else on earth has this privilege. No one else on earth has this responsibility. When we act as people of blessing, when you and I get off our donkeys and help people, we are keeping the covenant of what it means to be the people of God.

- *In his redemptive mission.* God is redeeming everything damaged and tainted by the entrance of sin into the world. Sin's devastation resulted in the alienation of people from God, from each other, from the rest of God's creation, even from themselves. Salvation is the reversal of this dilemma and the restoration of God's creation to its intended design. This mission is God's, not ours, because he is the only one with the power and ability to pull it off. Part of his strategy was the creation of the church. His mission gave birth to the church, not the other way around. Said another way, the church doesn't have a mission; the mission has a church.

> When we act as people of blessing, when you and I get off our donkeys and help people, we are keeping the covenant of what it means to be the people of God.

Kingdom enterprise is not a subset of church activity. Church activity is a subset of God's kingdom efforts.

Anything the church does that does not contribute to the kingdom is off mission. The Good Samaritan story highlights this distortion. A wrong focus by the priest and Levite caused them to pass by on the other side of the road instead of helping a needy person. It was the wrong side of the road!

- *In the world.* The world is where the mission of God plays out. "All the world's a stage" (to borrow a line from an "obscure" English author). It is the stage where God shows up and shows off. In his meeting with Nicodemus, Jesus said, "For God so loved the *world* that he gave his one and only Son" (John 3:16, emphasis added). Notice he did not say, "For God so loved the *church*." The church is not God's main focus; the world is. The world is on God's heart. This means that our spiritual journey as Jesus-followers should not lead us into more and more isolation from the world, cloistered away from its concerns. Being followers of Jesus means that we follow Jesus! When we do so, he leads us out into the streets. He expects to see us tracking with him as he engages people in the world to deliver life and hope.

Reflection: What three people will you bless this week?

_____

_____

_____

Doing Good to Others Is Good for You

We don't help others in order to save ourselves—that would be a selfish motive. But the truth is, one of the best things we can do for ourselves is to help somebody else. There is a direct connection between our helping others and our experiencing abundant life.

Remember, the backdrop to the Good Samaritan parable was the question, "What must I do to inherit eternal life?" (Luke 10:25). Jesus affirmed this personal concern by dealing with the man's quest very seriously. He said that the man was right in his understanding that loving God and loving our neighbors *as ourselves* is the ticket. "You have answered correctly. . . . Do this and you will live" (v. 28). Notice that Jesus pulled the man's search for eternal life into the present. The man considered eternal life as something that began after this life. Jesus took out the word *eternal* with his reply, simply declaring that if the man would follow his understanding, he would live. Life is today, right now.

> *As we move out of self-centeredness, self-consciousness, and self-absorption, we actually discover what we are seeking— to be truly alive!*

The key to experiencing life, according to Jesus in this exchange, is to love God and serve those who are needy. As we become givers of life, we receive life. As we lose ourselves, we find ourselves. As we move out of self-centeredness, self-consciousness, and self-absorption, we actually discover what we are seeking—to be truly alive! And in the process, the self we discover will be one we were created by God to be.

Reflection: How is the "love your neighbor" dynamic playing out in your life right now?

———————◆———————

By now you have figured out we are all in this story of the Good Samaritan. All of us are down and out in some way or another. Our needs can be physical, emotional, spiritual, or financial—and usually wind up being a combination of these. The needs of some Americans are more pronounced these days. In communities all across our country, people face huge challenges right now.

Let's be honest. We are also the people in the story who pass by on the other side of the road. We have all made that choice at one time or another. It reflects our need for salvation. We are captured by our own selfish interests to the point that we fail to respond to others' predicaments by helping them out.

Then I have one friend who jokes that he is probably the donkey in the story! (Maybe you have friends like that.)

But seriously and truthfully, there is a chance for all of us to be the hero in the story. If we reflect the heart of God, take action, and help people who need it, we become kingdom agents. It all starts by getting off our donkeys!

We have a choice to make. We are all on this road together. Which side are you on?

2

JUST PASSING BY

Just why do we pass by on the other side of the road when confronted with such obvious need? Let's acknowledge some factors that tend to keep us from making the right move.

Religious Activity

The priest and the Levite in the story represented leaders in the Jewish religious system of the first century. Priests offered various sacrifices central to Judaism and conducted other religious rites in the temple precincts in Jerusalem. Levites took care of the operational aspects of temple life, from preparing utensils for ritual use to maintaining the buildings and grounds. Together they were, in effect, the crew in charge of church services in Jesus's day.

If priests or Levites touched a dead person, they would be disqualified from active duty until they went through a purification process. The half-dead victim in Jesus's story presented a dilemma for the religious leaders. Maybe he already appeared dead, so they were afraid to approach him. Or if they tried to help and the man died on them, they would be religiously unclean. So they opted out of helping a dying man in order to preserve their ability to perform their religious duties!

Jesus's listeners would have been very familiar with these roles and rules. But by suggesting that people's needs have priority over religious observance, Jesus blew the cover off religion. He exposed the religious establishment's values and challenged its control over people's lives.

The second attack Jesus hurled at religion was more subtle but not less profound. When the religious expert asked, "Who is my neighbor?" (sounds a little like "Am I my brother's keeper?"), he revealed a religious penchant to look for loopholes and escape clauses. In first-century Pharisaic Judaism, *neighbor* had skillfully been rendered as referring only to those who were members of the Jewish religious club—no Samaritans allowed. With this interpretation, the responsibility to care for anyone outside the club had been eliminated. Jesus turned the question completely around by focusing on the people issue, not the religious definition of *neighbor.* "Who *acted* like a neighbor?" was his take on the situation. He reframed the question so no one could escape responsibility for how they displayed neighborliness.

It's easy for us to point fingers at first-century religious leaders. The problem is, religious activity is still getting in the way of our being good neighbors. The transgression is blatant; we just don't see it when we're caught up in it. What I'm talking about here is the stuff being done in the name of Jesus that puts meeting people's needs way down the list.

Religious charitable giving reaches almost one hundred billion dollars a year in the United States of America.[1] Is there any reason any child in America should go to sleep hungry or not have adequate school supplies (I could mention other societal ills) when the church is taking in billions of dollars a year? I'm just asking, but I already know the answer. You do too. We are consuming that money on religious enterprises and activities that have very little to do with Jesus or his concerns for the poor, the needy, the marginalized, the last, and the "least of these."

Following Jesus means being captured by what captures him. We have to ask ourselves: Are we acting neighborly? Are we helping anybody live a better life—here and now? This is what Jesus cares about. The litmus test of discipleship is "followship"! Are we *doing* what Jesus commanded, or are we just really good at recalling his commands?

> Are we **doing** what Jesus commanded, or are we just really good at recalling his commands?

Please don't hear what I am *not* saying. I am not against organized spiritual endeavors. I have spent my whole life engaged in these. I'm not remotely suggesting that you should shut church attendance or quit giving an offering to support church ministry. However, I am suggesting you take a close look at your time and energy (and money). If you are so involved in church that you don't have any margin of time or energy or money for people who need help, then it's more about religion than following Jesus. I'm also suggesting that you take a look at your charitable giving, whether to the church or to other places. Is it helping people live better lives? We have too many people bleeding out. Make sure your money is making it to "innkeepers" who are delivering actual help.

If you are a church leader, let me give you a warning. If you begin to shift your ministry agenda into the street to help people, the pushback will not come from the people you rescue. You will need courage to resist the demands of the religious crowd! They will clamor for more religious stuff, even wrap their consumerist addiction in spiritual language—anything to distract from their clear disobedience of passing by on the other side of the road.

But let me encourage you as well. The most fulfilled ministry leaders I am around today are the ones making the decision to lead their people into the streets of human need. That is because these leaders are pitching in with life and the kingdom. On the other hand, burnout and cynicism are the twin stalkers of leaders who have chosen just to be church-culture customer service reps. That's because religion's self-centeredness and self-absorption prevent it from delivering what it promises. It does not deliver life. Rather, it serves up more death masquerading as life.

Hell is the most religious place in the universe. Everyone there is very busy, but nobody is getting any help. Hell on earth—cloaked in religious activity— ain't far behind.

Reflection: How do you battle religion in your life?

_____

_____

_____

While religion might be the most sinister force that keeps us on our donkeys, it is by no means the only one. Let's take a look at others.

Judgmentalism and Prejudice

Judgmentalism and prejudice present two formidable barriers to our responding to human need that go hand in hand, reinforcing one another. Our negative judgments of people create prejudice and our prejudice causes us to judge others negatively. Both sustain the propensity to assess situations and the people in them in ways that relieve us of the responsibility to intervene: "It's their own fault." "That's what they get for being the way they are." "They're in this mess because of who they are." How much this played into the priest's and Levite's decisions in our Bible story is left for us to ponder.

Many factors feed these two impediments to our doing good. Some of us have had prejudices imprinted on us by our family of origin. We were raised from birth judging certain people as inherently inferior or deficient in ways we deem undesirable or unacceptable. These learned prejudices can manifest themselves blatantly (racism, for example) or in more subtle forms (social ostracism, classism). Perhaps we have been instructed by our religious training to see those holding alternative beliefs as "outsiders" or "others" unworthy of our help. Other biases can reflect social and economic prejudice. Our life experiences play into the formation of these opinions as well. The list of sources for our judgmentalism and prejudice can go on and on.

Judgmentalism and prejudice have been under cultivation since the Garden of Eden. As soon as Eve took her bite of the forbidden fruit, she experienced a separation not just from God but from Adam as well. This was a departure from the oneness the two had enjoyed up to that moment. Wanting him now to be like her, she persuaded him to take his own bite. This alienation from each other has proceeded unabated throughout human history. It is the cause of hostilities and wars, ethnic cleansing, racism, and all economic and social inequity. The presence of these twin phenomena cuts through all cultures, all classes, all people groups.

Our decision to pass by on the other side of the road is often informed and encouraged by these deeply ingrained evil twins. They lead us to categorize others ("That's just the way they are") and situations ("That's just the way it is") so we can dismiss them and scoot out from under any personal responsibility for getting involved.

Not long ago I was addressing a group about this very issue. One of the attenders told me after the event that in the previous week she had come face-to-face with her own biases and prejudice. In a ministry encounter with the homeless, she engaged a homeless man who declared to her how blessed he is and how Jesus is central to his life. "What I realized," she told me, "was that I had a stereotyped view of homeless people. This man's attitude of gratitude shattered my preconceptions."

Our judgmentalism and prejudice can make it easy for us to transfer responsibility to the victim for their plight. *If that guy had not been so foolish as to be on the Jerusalem-Jericho road, he wouldn't have been in this predicament. Everybody knows it's a dangerous highway, its mountainous twists and terrain harboring bands of thieves. And what was he doing out there by himself? He should have been traveling in a convoy. He should have studied martial arts so he could fight off an outnumbering force. Come to think of it, there are always people in trouble on that road. It's been dangerous going that way for centuries. If we help this guy out, we'll be encouraging others to take similar chances. We'll just be contributing to the problem!*

There is no doubt that some people who need our help are in situations they could have or should have avoided. But, also unquestionably, people are caught in social and economic situations that are beyond their control—or ours! Have we decided that people get what's coming to them? Or they should have been smarter? Or that's just the way it is with "those people" and "their situations"? Is assessing fault a way to escape our need to demonstrate compassion?

Playing the blame game is not an option left to us by Jesus. Will we let our judgmentalism and prejudice keep us perched on our donkeys?

Tom didn't. This friend of mine told me the story of moving into his new apartment with his wife and young school-age son. The first night as they lay down to sleep, loud music started up next door and continued until the wee hours of the morning. The next day Tom, his wife, and their son knocked on their neighbor's door, introduced themselves, and invited the man to dinner. Over dinner they learned that this neighbor had been abused and abandoned by both his parents by age five.

"My heart broke for him," Tom told me. "At that point my neighbor went from being a problem to being a person." Judgmentalism and prejudice wilted when hospitality opened the door for compassion to enter.

> Judgmentalism and prejudice wilted when hospitality opened the door for compassion to enter.

Admitting and addressing that we are judgmental or prejudiced is never fun or easy. But it is an essential aspect of our own personal and spiritual development. Our response to those suffering around us forces us to take a hard look at ourselves, to confront our own biases. While it is always easy to see the judgmentalism and prejudice others carry, it is usually more difficult to see them operating in us.

Reflection: What are some biases and prejudices keeping you on your donkey?

_____

_____

_____

Here's the deal. If you can't bring yourself to face these beasts—for whatever reason—that's still no excuse for you to stay firmly ensconced on your donkey. Deal with them later. Postpone the surgery if you're not ready. You don't have to fix yourself before getting in the game. In fact, I find that people often are moved to change their prejudices when they engage others' needs. When the problems we are addressing turn into people we care about, our biases and prejudices become challenged at a profound level.

So let's admit that all of us carry judgmentalism and prejudice around to some degree. And let's agree that we need to do some self-assessment to see if these are holding us back.

But do that on your own time. Right now your neighbor needs your help!

Busyness and Distraction

One of the really effective strategies of the enemy is to wear down God's people through exhausting lifestyles. This approach doesn't kill you all at once. It takes a little piece of your life away each day. It's like being nibbled to death by toothless piranhas. What's left over then suffers the debilitation of your energy, strength, and enthusiasm. The result is chronic tiredness, increased anxiety, and toxic stress levels. Lives filled full, but not "full-filled."

American culture is infested with epidemic levels of busyness. Preschoolers' schedules squeeze out playtime. School-age kids are lugged around to demanding after-school activities and programs before going home to face mountains of homework. Workers spend increasing amounts of time on the job, then bring their work home with them via their digital connections. Vacations get squeezed—not just for economic reasons, but because there is "so much to do!" Some wise cultural observer said that Western civilization will not blow up; it will just give out in a whimper, lie down, and die from exhaustion!

The implication for our discussion is that our level of busyness negatively impacts our capacity and willingness to get off our donkeys. I mean, who's got time to stop and help somebody who's broken down? We've got places to go and people to see. Our own donkey is hauling it as fast as it can, ears pinned back, braying, straining to get on up the road.

I am not about to take on the whole load of societal and personal sickness related to our overly stuffed, frenetic, and frantic lifestyles. That's a book or two in itself. But I want to flag this huge problem for us all rather than simply ignore the realities of American life. If we want to be more available to our neighbors in need, we will have to figure out some ways to increase the margins in our time and energy to make room for other people. It won't be easy.

I am reminded of one of my doctoral students. He and his wife made a huge lifestyle shift a few years ago that involved scaling back to create more margins in their lives for developing relationships and helping people. They sold their home in the burbs and moved into the inner city. This automatically saved them commute time (they both work in the city), allowing them to get home early enough to sit on their porch a minimum of three nights a week to strike up conversations with people who were out and about in the neighborhood. Plus the housing was cheaper, giving them more money to spend on service projects to bless their community. This young couple decided to be two fewer rats in the race and live more intentionally as people of blessing.

> *If we want to be more available to our neighbors in need, we will have to figure out some ways to increase the margins in our time and energy to make room for other people.*

The determination to become more engaged with the people in need in our communities might lead some of us to schedule some time, at a minimum, to be helpful to others. Blocking off an hour or two a week might be what it takes. Maybe that's the only way it will work for us. Others of us will be led to examine our lives from stem to stern, looking for radical ways to simplify so that more time is actually available for living and for helping others, which in turn enriches life. Finding more time for others can be a way to add to your own life fulfillment. I have rarely met people engaged in helping others who feel their lives lack meaning or purpose.

A societal ill related to that of busyness is distraction. There are so many opportunities, so many choices, so many things to do, our heads are spinning. And we don't even have to go anywhere! I'm talking just about the stuff on our smartphones or home computers. Some of us can remember when the Library of Congress couldn't be sucked out of thin air. People used to sit at meals engaged in conversation instead of being cut off from each other by listening to the music on their headsets. Believe it or not, people used to walk through malls looking at the shops and engaging other people rather than looking down at devices held in their hands.

We are so distracted by all we're up to, we miss the people around us. And their needs. We just don't notice. We heard something somewhere about a need for mentors at school, but where was that, anyway? Some public service announcement came on during the football game on television, but we were checking email and returning messages during the commercial. We're so caught up with all we've got going on, we have attention deficit disorder when it comes to tuning in to what's happening with other people—unless they text us.

Hey, having options for what to do with our lives is not going to decrease in intensity or go away. And I don't want it to. I like being able to decide when to do what. But if we are going to be available and helpful to others, we are simply going to have to pay more attention. We are going to have to figure out some way to focus ourselves long enough to meet other people's needs. Again, this decision will probably force some other decisions. It might even require that we give up some things that we discover are really just distractions anyway.

Busyness and distraction subtract from life. The way to add life back in is to become more intentional about how we're living. Making room to focus on other people is one important way we can do this. Once we introduce some disciplined serv ce into our lifestyles, many of us will enjoy the feeling that our lives are in less of a free fall. Once again, the life we save might be our own!

Reflection: What are your greatest challenges related to busyness and distraction?

_____

_____

_____

Being Overwhelmed

The big picture of need can overwhelm us to the point of paralysis. Hunger, poverty, illiteracy, unemployment—these problems are so huge that we feel hopeless to make any difference. Not just because of the scale of the issues but because of their complexity. It seems that once you wade into one area, you suddenly are confronted with three more challenges that are connected to the presenting problem. A schoolkid's failure to learn can be attributed to their being food-challenged, which results from poverty, which certainly is related to unemployment, which might result from adult illiteracy. All these categories have become institutionalized in our culture, with the sobering truth that some people are born into these conditions and never rise above them. The deck is stacked against them by their parents!

This cascading effect can make you feel that in your efforts to help, you're just sticking fingers in a dike. You ask yourself,

"What difference will it make?" which leads to "What's the use?" which leads to inaction. Overwhelmed by the need, you do nothing. Which, by the way, ensures the status quo.

I am sure you know where I am headed with this. We have to resist the forces that immobilize our yearnings to get involved in helping others. Scale the problem to one! If you help one kid learn to read, you may break the chain of poverty for that kid. And by increasing their life possibilities, you may actually influence generations to come for all those who follow them. Your efforts may reduce the prison population by one, take one person off food stamps, or help one person become employable. You can bring hope to one person who otherwise stares at a landscape of lifelong despair.

One. Resist the notion that it doesn't matter, that it won't make a difference. It matters to that *one* you help. And you, as one, might start a movement that never would have materialized without your initiative.

You might discover that once you get moving, you will find the energy, the resources, and the capacity to go to two, then ten, fifty, a hundred, maybe a thousand. Perhaps some people will join you in what you're doing. Some others will write checks. A few can commit entire organizations of resources.

You never know how what you do might capture the imagination of a whole community. Just this morning I received a Facebook message from Bethany, a woman who attended a presentation I gave four years ago, during which I shared the backpack food program idea. The kids we feed in schools during the week go home to food-challenged environments for the weekend, so the backpack program sends food home with those kids.

Here's what Bethany wrote: "You made one comment about a weekend backpack food program for children, and I felt God telling me, 'This is it!' So I began a few months later serving 19 children at our school. . . . God has grown this movement to us being in 35 schools today in 13 different districts reaching 1,500 children." Then she added, "Entire communities and schools are coming together because of this." Bethany wrote to thank me for the idea, not even realizing that *she* is the hero in the story. She's the *one* who did something.

I am also thinking of two other people right now, each of whom became passionate about an issue in their communities. One lives in a small town, the other in a large city. Both have galvanized hundreds of people, and one has raised hundreds of thousands of dollars, the other millions, to address their issues. Both are determined to re-create the future for hundreds and thousands of people in their communities. Neither had any idea when they started that they would instigate the movement they are seeing.

> *You never know how what you do might capture the imagination of a whole community.*

You know what? They didn't get involved by relying on others. They had a passion that would not let them sit on the sidelines anymore.

It all starts with one.

In the story that Jesus told, the Good Samaritan didn't chase down the robbers, reengineer the road to be less likely to harbor criminals, or work for greater police protection on the highway. Neither did the good neighbor pick up every other broken-down or needy person on the road. But he did help one.

And that one mattered.

Reflection: Who or what is the "one" for you?

_____

_____

_____

Fear

Let's just go ahead and call this one out. Fear keeps a bunch of us from crossing the road to make a difference.

Fear comes in all sizes and shapes. Insecurity, fear of failure, threatened safety, fear of being incompetent or not up to the challenge, fear of what the costs will be to our resources, or fear of being taken advantage of—any or all these fears, plus others that might be customized for each of us, often plague us to the point that we shrink back from offering ourselves as part of the solution to others' needs.

I have three things to say about fear. First, let's talk about its source. Have you ever wondered where fears come from? They come from the enemy of life. When we give in to fear, we die a little. Remember part of an old maxim: cowards die a thousand deaths. It's true. Fear robs us of life. And it robs others of theirs too!

God gets this. He understands how fear stalks us all. That is why the most frequent instruction in the Bible is "Don't be afraid!" Often that phrase is accompanied by the promise "I am with you." For those who know God, the connection between the two statements makes great sense. When he is around (and he always is), we are surrounded by love. His love. Perfect love. The good news is, "Perfect love drives out fear" (1 John 4:18).

This doesn't mean bad things won't happen to us. They do. We all get sick and die. Some of us get beat up pretty badly on the road before we die. But for those aware of God's presence, these experiences are less terrifying. That may not seem like much consolation. But consider this: we all go through pain, suffering, heartache, and disappointment. We can add fear to every experience, or we can take fear out of the equation. That's where the promise of the presence of God comes in. We face none of this stuff alone.

The enemy of your soul whispers fear to you whenever he can. That never comes from God. And now that you know where fear comes from, it doesn't have to be an inevitable companion on your journey. Every occurrence or flash of fear can be rescripted in your mind as a reminder that you are not alone, that God is with you. It wouldn't be surprising to me if when you begin to use attacks of fear as reasons to remember God's love for you, the attacks subside. Satan doesn't get his jollies by reminding you of God's goodness.

Here's the second point I want to make about fear: it always comes on as larger than it is. Fear caroms off the corridors of our mind, its echoes making it seem even scarier as the reverberations amplify in our spirit.

I remember standing over a paper bag years ago, poised with golf club in hand, waiting for an unknown thing to show itself and finally come out of the bag. Its rustling had alerted my wife and me to its presence and to the dread that something had invaded the closet in our bedroom. Wanting to protect my new bride and prove myself brave, I grabbed the only weapon I had—a 9 iron. Closer and closer the bag monster came to the top of the sack. Suddenly it appeared—a bug! With ten thousand legs scratching the stiff paper sack, it had sounded ferocious. It proved far less formidable when I got a good look at it. It was no match for my 9 iron! (Neither was the carpet. I never have been that accurate with a golf club.)

> Every occurrence or flash of fear can be rescripted in your mind as a reminder that you are not alone, that God is with you.

Fear is like that. It scratches and burrows, whispers and shouts, raising quite a ruckus in our souls. That whiff of uncertainty we sense in early afternoon reaches gale-force strength by bedtime. We struggle to sleep because of certain impending doom. That nagging doubt tugging at our attention becomes a central concern, suddenly causing us to question everything we thought we knew. A simple note of discord ramps up its volume until every other song is drowned out except the symphony of fear.

Fear struts. It postures. It intimidates. It has to, because in the end—and this is the third thing I want to say about fear—it has no teeth. Fear hides in the shadows so you can't see how powerless it really is.

Face your fear. Pull that puppy out into the full light of day. You will be amazed how it shrinks and curls up into a fetal position.

Now let's apply these insights to our broader discussion of why we fail to help others when they so obviously need it. Fear tells us that if we try to help other people, they will just take advantage of us. Fear tells us that we will just enable people in their poor choices, so we will be doing more harm than good. Fear tells us that we are going to run into needs we can't meet.

America does not need to marry fear; heck, we don't even need to date it. Those who fear that our future is bleak play right into the story line that fear concocts. Its tale is not an unavoidable reality. It is a myth.

Write a different ending. Kick fear in the donkey.

Reflection: What fears do you face? What feeds them?

Indifference and Apathy

I want to call attention to one other barrier that keeps us from being good neighbors. Indifference and apathy prevent many people from getting involved with their community of need. So I want to make a couple of points.

First, it really is true that indifference and apathy not only tolerate but often encourage persistent problems that should not be sustained. Recently I told a group of church leaders in one city that their community has an illiteracy problem—not because of a failing educational system, but because of a failure of the church. I said the same thing about hunger. Hunger persists not because of a failure of government programs but because of a failure of the church to step convincingly into that space.

Now, I am not naive. These are real problems, and very real institutions have indeed let us down. And there are more players to be considered than just church people. But I was trying to make the point to that crowd—and now to you—that the willingness of the church to tolerate poverty, hunger, and illiteracy has contributed to the persistence of these conditions. This is the United States of America, for crying out loud. A land of resources and opportunity. A land of talent and expertise. A land of freedom and choice. We don't have to wait for anybody to fix our country. We—you and I—should fix it. If enough people in that crowd that I was speaking to will get off their donkeys, the number of kids going hungry at school will go down and the number of kids with good reading grades will go up!

Second, no matter what reason or reasons lead us to decide to stay on our donkeys, by doing so we send a signal of indifference and apathy. That's how it comes across to the people who are suffering. "We don't care enough to do anything about it" is what our inactivity says to them.

---◆---

I don't really care why you are still on your donkey at this point. I just want you to get off it and get going. Hopefully this chapter has lit a fuse under your . . . intentions.

53

"But I don't know what to do," I hear some of you saying. Funny you should ask. The answer to your question might surprise you. The information you need to get started doesn't lie "out there" somewhere.

As you'll see in the next chapter, it begins with you!

3

HELP YOURSELF

Harvey is a retired gentleman who volunteered last year to become a mentor in a local middle school through a tutoring program started by his congregation. His mentoree is John, a young man who had failed eighth grade. It was at that point that Harvey entered the young man's life. Not only has John now finished eighth grade with As and Bs, he's knocking the ball out of the park in ninth grade.

Harvey meets John every Monday morning before school. To say they have become tight friends is too anemic a description. Harvey couldn't even talk to me about his relationship with John without tearing up. When I said that he was obviously making a tremendous contribution to John's life, Harvey began shaking his head side to side. With tears streaming down his face and his lips quivering, he croaked, "What he's doing for me is so much more than anything I'm doing for him!"

Do yourself a favor. Get off your donkey and help somebody. You won't just be helping them; you will be giving yourself a big break. Because when you help others, you help yourself!

The episode leading into the story of the Good Samaritan begins with a question of self-interest. "What must *I* do to inherit eternal life?" the religious teacher asked.

Jesus's response included the admonition for us to love our neighbors the way *we love ourselves*. Your motivation for loving others, according to Jesus, should reflect the same kind of interest and concern that you have for yourself. But don't forget the reward, which was the point of the exchange—eternal life. As we have seen, in Jesus's view that means a better life beginning here and now. And that means your own path to a more fulfilling life runs squarely into the land of helping others.

Jesus is not the only one who has made the connection between serving others and having an improved self. Gallup research scientists have identified "Community Wellbeing" as one of five essential elements of a person's well-being.[2] These scientists observe:

> At the highest end of the Community Wellbeing continuum is giving back to society. When we asked people with thriving wellbeing about the greatest contribution they had made in their life, with few exceptions, they mentioned the impact they have had on another person, group, or community.[3]

These authors conclude that this sense of having made a contribution "may be what differentiates an *exceptional* life from a good one" (emphasis added).[4] Jesus would call this the abundant life (see John 10:10).

I am not suggesting that we help others in order to help ourselves; that would be self-serving, not others-serving. But it has been my experience that people who help others find themselves benefited in many ways. The payoff may not match their gift in kind (they may give money but receive emotional reward), but it always exceeds their contribution in the sense of satisfaction that it brings.

The paradoxical truth is that the quickest way to self-improvement might just be to improve someone else's life. Doing good to others constitutes a form of self-development. And as we improve ourselves more, we actually are better able to help others. Both actions—loving our neighbors and loving ourselves— can be mutually reinforcing. You become the person God wants you to be as you help others. And as you become more of who you are, you are better able to love your neighbor.

> Both actions—loving our neighbors and loving ourselves— can be mutually reinforcing.

The dynamic interplay between these two themes is what we are exploring together in this book. The first two chapters have focused on motivating you to help others. If you were to put the book down now and just do that, the world would be better and that would be good. But I hope you keep reading. Because there is something more in this for you too. So far I have focused on the need of your neighbor; now I'm flipping the conversation around to focus on your personal development. But I'm going to have this conversation through the filter of helping others. Along the way I will comment on how your personal development can and does inform the way you are available to help your neighbor.

To help you see what I mean, let's take a look in this chapter at just some of the gifts we ourselves receive from serving others.

Greater Self-Awareness

One of the key benefits of serving others will be your own increased self-awareness. I contend that the most important body of information you must possess is your own self-awareness. Self-awareness allows you to avoid self-centeredness and self-absorption. It allows you to bring a more informed and better *you* to the life you are making for yourself and for others.

People with self-awareness possess valuable insights about themselves that inform their contributions to others. Their efforts are fueled by their passions and values, which they have sorted out. This, in turn, allows them to be more intentional about what it is they are trying to accomplish. In addition, knowing what competencies they bring to the table helps self-aware people craft their contributions, not overpromising or underdelivering on what they can do. Their self-knowledge also improves the health of their relationships. They don't value others merely for what they gain from them. They invest in other people because they have a desire for helping others experience a better life.

Nothing accelerates this self-awareness like efforts to help others. In serving other people, we are brought face-to-face with our motivations, our limitations, our likes and dislikes, our biases and prejudices, our strengths, our dark sides, our passions, our weaknesses, our boundaries—a whole range of self-awareness issues.

In my own efforts to help others, I have found out a lot of things about myself. Some insights I'm not too proud of. But these discoveries have helped me to make some positive changes. For instance, I have found that sometimes I frustrate people rather than help them. My "encouragement" for them to make better decisions sometimes doesn't come across that way. Sometimes I actually make people feel less capable and competent. My mistake usually involves assigning to others my own set of motivational factors, which they may or may not have. This bit of insight has helped me become more sensitive (on occasion) and more customized in my approach. On the positive side, my engagement with others to help them has helped me see that when I do get it right, people are moved to achieve great things that they didn't know or believe they could do (psst, I'm hoping to do that with you!).

Your increased self-awareness will support every aspect of your service to others. It will help you know what to do—and what not to do. At the same time, wise investments of your passions, energies, and talents into helping others will help you become more of who you are meant to be. Here again, helping others is a way to be good to yourself—you get to know yourself better!

Better Connection with People

While traveling through the countryside of the south island of New Zealand a few years ago, I came across a sign propped up against a sheep farmer's mailbox on the side of the road. On a large sheet of plywood, someone had stenciled a profound message. It read simply, "ONE:WE." I have no idea what prompted this New Zealander to create such a powerful statement. But in my mind, those two words capture the essence of human community. There is no *we* without *me*, and there is no *me* without *we*. We're all in this together.

Human beings alone out of all creation share the unique bond of being created in the image of God. This fundamental identity connects us all. Each and every person on our planet deserves consideration because of this relationship. The neighbor out of work is a person created in the image of God. The child whose stomach growls through the night is a special creation of God, supremely valued by him and dignified through the gift of his image. The fabulously wealthy are just as truly special—not for their riches, but because they too share the image of God. Their needs may not be financial, but they can be just as emotionally and psychologically needy as anyone.

The fact that we are all created in the image of God inherently tasks us for others' well-being. That's a fancy way of saying that all people matter to God, and they should matter to us!

We are moved to care for others because we share God's image with them. That's the point of connection. The image of a trinitarian God (ONE:WE indeed!) has built into us a yearning for community, for connectedness with other human beings and with God.

Unfortunately, there are too few people with the ONE:WE perspective. It seems that most often we run into another sign—an ancient one we just won't let go of. "US:THEM" could have been the sign erected right outside Eden's gate to commemorate the fall. Unfortunately, that message has been carried from that moment on into every culture. It is the most immediate consequence of that sin event—the estrangement from others and our God. And it is the most predominant sign displayed on the mailboxes of humanity. We all figure out how to turn others into "them" instead of "we." Once we categorize people this way, we can ignore "them," hate "them," and kill "them," all the while thanking God we are not like "them." Selfishness, hoarding, walling off, holding back, not caring—these are the telltale manifestations that we are all descended from Eden's cataclysm. But while prevalent, this condition of fractured relationships is not normal. In fact, we must consider it abnormal to our created design.

When we live up to our best self, the self that God is redeeming and re-creating in Jesus, we are pulled out of our default position of self-centeredness into caring for others. We are motivated to get off our donkeys because God calls out to us through every other human being we meet. Among the gifts of serving others, then, is that we ourselves find our place of belonging.

Being Blessed as People of Blessing

In chapter 1 I mentioned that the people of God have the special assignment to bless the world. The church has stepped into Abraham's story—and his covenant. The church is part of the ongoing incarnational presence of God's blessing strategy for and in the world. Loving our neighbors as ourselves is another way of saying that our job is to bless the people we come in contact with. When we act as people of blessing, we live up to our covenant as the people of God.

But we *ourselves* are also blessed by being people of blessing.

All around the country at church gatherings, I share the message that we are to be people of blessing. As I do, I am treated with stories of people whose lives are transformed by this understanding of who they are as the people of God and what they are supposed to be doing in this world.

> Loving our neighbors as ourselves is another way of saying that our job is to bless the people we come in contact with.

"This is such a *fun* way to live," many consistently say. "When I intentionally bless people, it opens up all kinds of spiritual conversations," others say. "This is so simple—and so freeing," is another comment I often get. And almost always I hear, "*I* am being blessed way more than anything I'm passing on to others."

The people who share how rewarding it is to bless others have come alive because they are living the life God intended for them. By blessing others, they are being blessed. Through their efforts in helping others, they are helping themselves.

Good News Leads to Good Works

You were created *on* purpose *for* a purpose. The reason God created you is to give you the life he wants you to have, to share his life with you. Your purpose, then, is to share that life with those around you, including and especially with those who need the blessings of the life you enjoy. This involves both telling people *good news* about God's gift for them as well as doing *good works* to demonstrate that gift.

God intentionally connected good news and good works with the element that guides all of your relationship with him: faith. If you are a Jesus-follower, you entered that relationship through faith. You also grow into your purposeful good works through faith. How so? To discover the good works God has planned for you, you have to seek God's mind and will about what you are to do. This process of inquiry and discovery builds your faith muscles as you interact with God. It is his way of keeping your need for him front and center in your life.

One of my colleagues likes to say that God has two questions and two answers for us. The answers to the two questions can't be interchanged. Neither works to answer the other question. God's first question, "Why should I let you into heaven?" can only be addressed with the truth of Ephesians 2:8–9: "For it is by grace you have been saved, through faith—and this is not from yourselves, it is the gift of God—not by works, so that no one can boast." God's second question to us, "What did you do with the life I gave you?" finds its response in verse 10: "For we are God's handiwork, created in Christ Jesus to do good works, which God prepared in advance for us to do." We don't earn our salvation—Jesus does that. But when it comes to the stewardship of our lives, we can't offer up Jesus's work on our behalf. God expects us to *do* something with what we have received. In other words, sitting smugly on our donkeys with our ticket punched to heaven doesn't cut it for what God had in mind when he gifted us with salvation.

This is not so difficult to understand. If we give a car to someone who needs a car, we would be shocked if they just left

> Sitting smugly on our donkeys with our ticket punched to heaven doesn't cut it for what God had in mind when he gifted us with salvation.

62

it parked. Even if they displayed the car prominently, washed and waxed it every Sunday, wrote songs of gratitude to us, and told all their friends about our generosity, we would still be frustrated if they didn't use the car. We would not take back the gift (after all, it was a gift), hoping that they would someday figure out why we gave them the car. Yet every week the car sat idle. we would wonder why and wish the recipient would get the full benefit of the gift we gave them.

The good news is that the good works God intends for you and me to do are not something or some things we have to invent. They were prepared "in advance" by God for us, just like our salvation was.

Self-Discovery

Connect the Dots was one of my favorite puzzles when I was a kid. I really enjoyed watching an image emerge as I drew lines between the numbered connection points. Some puzzles had a few lines already drawn in, offering some clues to the final object. Sometimes I could guess pretty quickly what I was drawing; on other occasions I was surprised at what took shape. No matter the case, I could proceed with confidence because I was guaranteed to figure out what was initially hidden as long as I connected the dots the right way.

Of course, your life is a puzzle way more complicated than these childhood drawings. The dots are not always obvious, and they certainly don't come sequentially laid out for you. But if you connect the right dots, you can figure out who you are, what you should be doing, and what contributions you want to make—all the important issues that come together for a meaningful life.

The dots are the key pieces of your life that need to be connected. If you can identify them and figure out how they go together, you can move forward with confidence that your life will come together. You don't have to know the final design to get started—that's the point of working the puzzle! You just need to know that you are working on the right set of questions and issues that help you become the *you* that God intended.

In the chapters ahead, we will isolate and explore some of these key dots in your life. Discovering your life mission, clarifying what is really important to you, identifying what you are good at, figuring out what you need to learn, and building a scorecard that supports all of the above—I believe these are massively important issues that impact every area of our lives. As we investigate these key questions, you will not just get a better idea about how you can serve others with your life; you will also get greater insights into who you are.

Discovering We Are Built to Serve!

Recently I had a conversation with a young man who is mentoring schoolkids in the poorest and most crime-ridden part of his city. Talk about challenging! The apartment complex Harry works in has had multiple murders in the past twelve months alone. It took over a year of his being in that community for the parents of the kids to trust him. Harry spends at least ten hours a week working with his own mentorees. In addition, he is raising money and recruiting volunteers for an after-school program he dreams of establishing that will change both the destination and the destiny for the kids in this area.

This young professional does all this on top of his work and family responsibilities. As I listened to his story, I asked him, "Aren't you exhausted?"

He answered, "There's good tired and bad tired." Then, with a smile, he added, "My work with the kids is a good tired. *This is what I am meant to do*" (emphasis added).

You could no more talk this young man out of his engagement with this passion than you can halt the setting of the sun. I have known Harry for several years. I have watched him go through jobs and relationships in search of himself. Prior to our coffee shop conversation, I had lost touch with him for about two years. I was amazed at the transformation that had come over him during the intervening months. Some would argue that Harry is just maturing, and that is partly true. But I am convinced he has grown as he has gone beyond himself to be a person of blessing. Harry has come alive through this very challenging service to his community.

> *If we do not exercise our serving muscles, our souls will be undernourished.*

We are built to serve! The people I run into who are serving in their communities have a zest for life that spills out into every area of their lives. Conversely, people who stay on their donkeys miss the rewards of serving their neighbors. If we do not exercise our serving muscles, our souls will be undernourished.

Accelerated Spiritual Growth

The way of service as the path to discipleship is usually not emphasized in our American church culture. Making a big deal out of loving our neighbors might be reserved for a special emphasis every now and then, but everyday discipleship is mostly cast as a personal quest for God through various kinds of personal spiritual practices. The consumption of spiritual goods—whether it is worship, Bible study, prayer, fasting, giving—is mostly engaged in a congregational setting or as part of a church program. Discipleship has come to be measured as faithful participation in these church activities.

Good works done for others in arenas outside the church are not celebrated much as part of the path to discipleship. As a result, people don't see all of life as a discipling platform.

This compartmentalized view of discipleship paints spiritual development as an activity pursued apart from normal life. Truth is, if our spiritual growth doesn't show up in how we relate to others, run our businesses, treat our schoolmates, and deal with our neighbors, then it's not very spiritual. Spiritual development does not occur in some kind of vacuum. It works its way out in these relationships that are part of everyday life.

Here's an example of what I mean. A few years back, Cathy, my wife, was heavily involved in helping a mother of quintuplets (in addition to the one-year-old and seven-year-old sons this woman already had). Helping, in this case, meant whatever needed to be done, from rounding up food and baby equipment to remodeling a house to create enough room for the family. This was all on top of providing emotional and spiritual support to this overwhelmed and poverty-challenged young mom.

One day Cathy got a phone call from a well-meaning church lady who offered to begin mentoring the woman. She proposed coming by the home one day a week and taking Susan, the mom, out for a few hours' break and doing a Bible study with her. Cathy's immediate response was, "Why don't you come over and fold clothes and change diapers?" Then she added, "When Susan and I are doing laundry together, we talk about everything." The church lady's response to spiritual formation was to create an artificial environment, study some curriculum, and send Susan back to "plug and play" with whatever insights had been generated. Her motive was good, but her idea was inadequate because most people don't learn that way. Cathy's approach, on the other hand, involved relational and life-focused dynamics, anchored in normal life routines.

Serving other people is the quickest way to grow spiritually. It is the path to discipleship applauded by Jesus in his command that we should love our neighbors as ourselves.

Finding God

A knock on my office door one Sunday morning was followed by the entrance of a man I had come to know in my brief time as interim pastor of a congregation near my home.

"Can we talk a minute?" he asked as he sat down. "I need your help."

"Of course," I replied, wondering what might be the problem. Curiously, he began with a litany of his service to the church—serving on important committees, giving leadership as an elder, teaching adult Bible classes; the list went on and on. It was an impeccable résumé in terms of church member involvement and support. I thought he was providing this historical information as background. As it turned out, it was part of the problem. He summed up his dilemma this way: despite having done all these things for years, he said, "I'm missing something somewhere."

"Could it be *God* that you're missing?" I responded. I then pointed out to him that not one time in his description of his church life had he even mentioned God or Jesus! My observation shocked him, but he quickly agreed. He admitted that he didn't feel particularly close to God. And that's really what he was after.

Maybe, like him, you are one of the millions of churchgoers who keep wondering what's missing in their life. You have attended services, tithed, given to the building campaign, served on committees, worked with young people, and gone beyond the call of duty by serving as chaperone for middle school summer camp! Yet you have this nagging sense of unfulfillment. You are wondering when this abundant life that you were promised—if you would just participate more in church stuff—is going to kick in.

Unfortunately, you got the message that the church is Jesus's preferred hangout and that the world is a spiritually hostile wasteland. Predictably, then, you centered your search for God in church activities and church real estate. It seemed church was God's favorite place, where he loved to show off in the stained glass, the music, the liturgy, and the sermon. Hanging out with church people was the secret to becoming less and less like the world and more and more like Jesus.

> You might or might not meet God at church, but you are **guaranteed** to run into him where people need him desperately.

It seems to me we've had it backwards. The world has always been God's playground. The only question has been whether or not he is welcome at church! Jesus didn't drive money-changers out of the streets, after all. It was the temple they had corrupted. The temple had been overrun by religious programming and institutional operating concerns. Jesus was really ticked that a place where people were supposed to be able to find God had become a venue for temple marketing and income, obscuring God's face and derailing the chance to engage him.

So here's my suggestion for you in your search for God: get outside more. Get in the streets. You might or might not meet God at church, but you are *guaranteed* to run into him where people need him desperately. Mother Teresa used to speak of seeing the face of God in the faces of the poor of Calcutta. But you don't have to go to India to see him. You will find God in hospital emergency rooms, school cafeterias, homeless shelters, battered women's homes, soup kitchen lines, the unemployment office, bus stops—wherever people are hurting.

When we look after the welfare of others, we promote and participate in God's kingdom work. When we engage ourselves with a kingdom agenda, we are brought into contact with the King! People who help their neighbors are positioned to see God.

And when it comes to being good to yourself, it doesn't get any better than hanging out with God!

Renewal through Serving "in the Name of Jesus"

It is okay to serve people in the name of Jesus!

Years ago, during a break in a conference in California where I was speaking on ways congregations can be engaged more with their communities, a woman came up to me and told me part of her life story. "I am recently retired," she said. "I worked as an emergency room nurse for years, so I saw it all. But what sticks out in my mind is those years when we first began to see AIDS patients coming into the hospital. They didn't know what was wrong with them and we didn't know either. The young men were terrified! Many of them had lost contact with their families because of their lifestyle choices." She paused, then added, "Back then, being gay was much less openly talked about, so many of them had had their communication with their families severed. Here they were—scared and dying—and they felt they couldn't even share their circumstances with their families. Many of them didn't know how their families would react to hearing from them. It just broke my heart."

At this point the nurse's eyes teared up. "So I began to offer to do two things for them. One was to call their families for them. And the other was to offer to pray *with* them. In every case except one, these young men welcomed my prayers—and they all welcomed my assistance calling home. When I prayed with them, I talked to them about Jesus. No one objected. So I know we can minister to other people in Jesus's name—if we are willing to enter their pain and suffering."

She then gave me the backstory on this part of her life journey. Her husband had suddenly died some years back. "I spent years asking God to give me another husband and complaining about my loneliness. One day I clearly heard God tell me, 'Give yourself to the people around you and let me fill your loneliness.' That was when I began my ministry to AIDS patients. By doing that, it took away my heartache." Smiling, she said, "God doesn't always give us what we want, but he gives us what we need."

I believe this woman would tell you to be good to yourself—give yourself to the people in need around you.

But let's return to the earlier point of my telling you this story. This emergency room nurse found no trouble integrating her service with her belief system. I think we can all be instructed by her. For a bunch of reasons, many of us Jesus-followers are too embarrassed to mention Jesus when we are serving people, feeling that it's the wrong thing to do. The result of this reluctance is that people are left with a caricature of Jesus that has been painted by some religious nut or poor church experiences or the media. People who need Jesus are not being introduced to him! People are underserved because they have not heard and understood the good news he brings.

I know where some of the retreat from being openly identified as a Jesus-follower comes from. We want to disassociate ourselves from those who imperiously announce their religious convictions by bullhorning people with bad news or challenging people about their life choices without stopping to serve them. Honestly, we don't need any more of this misguided and abusive approach.

But I think we've gone too far the other direction. People expect you and me to have some sort of belief system. They just don't want us to cram it down their throats. As we serve people, we should not pull back from sharing our best with them. We should be able to identify the reason for the hope that we have in us (1 Pet. 3:15). People deserve to know how much Jesus cares for them and the full measure of life he wants for them. That information, coming from someone who is being a servant to them, shows up in the right packaging.

Please hear me right on this. Serving people purely for the chance to share the gospel with them does not fit any biblical mandate. That approach reduces the love of neighbor into an act with an ulterior motive. It smacks of disingenuous service— and people can smell it a zip code away. People deserve to be loved for all the reasons we have already gone over, starting with their being created in the image of God. Help-

> People deserve to know how much Jesus cares for them and the full measure of life he wants for them.

ing people who need to be helped and doing good to others have value in and of themselves. After all, in the Bible story told by Jesus himself, the Samaritan didn't try to convert the person he helped.

I believe, however, that we are not availing ourselves of enough opportunities to connect our motives to Jesus. It's okay to obey him and serve him by serving people in our lives. And I think it's okay for them to know it, especially when they bring it up. And I think they *will* bring it up. Doing good deeds eventually leads to a discussion of motives and beliefs. We do not have to shy away at that point from sharing our own experience.

Also, serving people in Jesus's name will bring *you* renewed joy and energy. Sharon, who works in a food bank, learned this secret last year. All day long she interviews people to determine their needs and how her organization can help with their food challenges. She is passionate about this, but the day-in and day-out exposure to people's challenges was taking its toll on her. She began to ask people at the conclusion of their interview, "Can I pray *with* you?" Not only did she find that people really want her to pray for them and with them, she also discovered a new enthusiasm inside herself. People even write to her telling her they appreciate the food assistance, but they appreciate her prayers more! Sharon unashamedly prays "in Jesus's name." It has helped her believe all over again in the power of Jesus to touch people's lives.

◆

You've gotten the point. Helping others comes with a guaranteed self-help benefit. Not only does it move us out of our self-absorption, but loving our neighbor helps us get in touch with our own life purpose and with the God who made us and loves us and wants us to experience life to the max.

There are so many options, so many needs, so many people who are down in the dirt. How do we know where to start? How can you make your best contribution?

Again, the answer lies in you.

Reflection: How would you like to grow as a person? How can serving others help you with that?

4

THE MEANING OF LIFE

My daughters each had a cat when they were growing up. The animals didn't strike me as particularly thoughtful. The only thing the cats contemplated, I'm pretty sure, was how to increase my allergic reactions to them. Otherwise they took the days as they came—sleeping most of the time. We now have two Yorkshire terriers. They are barking in the other part of the house right now, convinced they are terrorizing the squirrels who are playing in the side yard. As opposed to the cats, the dogs will come when called. But I would have to say that the dogs show no more propensity for philosophical meditation than did the cats.

Human beings, on the other hand, seem to be uniquely afflicted with the quest for meaning. Everyone from Socrates to Billy Crystal has been looking for the meaning of life. People look to their parents, their teachers, their pastors, their friends, their therapists—to anyone who might have an idea. The desire to understand the reason for our being is a fundamental part of what it means to be human.

Could this haunting quest itself provide some sort of clue to life's meaning? I think it does. "Cosmic accidents" would have no rationale to search for a reason for being. But we are not here accidentally. We are here by design. And because we are, we ask for meaning. When we ask, "Why?" we assert meaning over randomness. Meaning implies intentionality. Intentionality implies design. Design begs for a designer. I believe that an intelligent Designer stands behind the universe. And behind you.

The nagging question of your life's mission points you beyond yourself to your designer. To God. When you search for life, you search for him. When you discover the reason for your life, your mission, you will discover God right in the big middle of it!

Since you are an intentional creation of God, this means you don't create your life's mission; you discover it! When you adopt this perspective, life becomes a journey of discovery, an adventure into meaning and personal mission.

Serving others contributes to our life's purpose in two very important ways. First, it provides significant opportunities for us to express our life passions. Just yesterday a guy wrote to me updating me on a career change he is making. He wants to serve leaders by providing personal coaching. His career move is designed to bring him into alignment with his desire to help leaders. By positioning himself to be more available to other people he wants to serve, he is making room for more intentional expression of his own major life passion.

Second, the changes that take place in us when we are serving others can also provide important clues into what our life mission is. They can help us figure out what we want to contribute to the world. Through the experiences of helping others, we discover what situations tug at our heartstrings or help us come alive or cause us to reorient our talents and priorities.

For example, I asked my friend Jeff, "Why do you feel pulled toward working with fatherless young boys?"

He replied, "When one of the young kids I was tutoring gave me four different answers to who his dad was, it broke my heart. I realized this boy wanted a dad so bad he was inventing one." He concluded, "That's when I decided somebody needed to take this kid under his wing and provide some male influence in his life." Jeff would not have made this self-discovery if he had not been involved in an after-school mentoring program. The experiences of serving in that program are now giving shape to Jeff's life purpose.

> *Figuring out your life's mission will help you better know how to serve others. At the same time, the work of serving others can help you figure out your life mission.*

These two related truths serve as a backdrop to this chapter's discussion. Figuring out your life's mission will help you better know how to serve others. At the same time, the work of serving others can help you figure out your life mission. Then you will know the meaning of life: it is a mission trip.

Here are a couple things to keep in mind as you start your investigation into your life mission. First, God is already at work in your life. The fact that you may not recognize this yet or are unable to understand it has not kept him away from you. You have never been off his screen. He is plotting to bring you abundant life.

Second, if your life currently is a mystery to you, it doesn't have to stay that way. God has dropped into your life some big clues to help you discover your life mission.

Passion

You get really excited about some things. They might be certain causes or particular activities or great dreams. Whatever

75

these passions are, they create energy in you. When they come up, you get fired up!

Recently I talked with a young musician who is just breaking into the market in his particular genre of music. Brad has recently signed with a record label, opening up lots of new opportunities for himself. I was interested in and asked about the various aspects of the recording contract, the sales projections, and expectations of the record producers. He answered these questions with lackluster enthusiasm.

Then we popped in a DVD of one of his recent concerts. He and I watched him perform two or three songs that Brad identified as his favorites.

"This is terrific stuff!" I told him.

Much more animated now, he gushed, "I love what I do!" Then he went on to describe the thrill of performing, of being on stage and feeling the energy in the room. Life sparkled through him as he talked about seeing people enjoy his music. The difference in his voice and demeanor told me that our discussion had now tapped into his passion.

Passion doesn't always have to feel like a fireworks display (or a concert performance). It can just as easily be manifested by a quiet conviction that fuels a person's determination. Passion might move an individual to engage street kids who have been abandoned by everyone else. It might cause a researcher to work late into the night looking for the cure for a disease. Passion keeps a person on task long after everyone else has given up.

People with passion stand out from other people who are involved in the same work or activity but don't have a passion for it. For the latter, it's just a job or something they've been assigned to. For the people operating from passion, it is an expression of who they are and what makes them tick.

Here's another example. My wife had to move both of her parents into a special-care Alzheimer's unit in their final days. They lived in another city, so her personal visits with them were days apart. But she checked on them regularly over the phone. There was one nurse Cathy loved to talk to when she called to check on her mom and dad. The reason had to do with the caregiver's passion. "I just *love* being here," she had told Cathy during an earlier visit. And it showed! While many of us (if not most) would recoil from dealing with mentally challenged people all day long, this lady actually looked forward to it. That's what passion does for you.

Some people, like that nurse, express their passion through their job or vocation. It's great when those line up like that. But it doesn't work that way for many of us. Our day jobs may be nothing more than ways we pay the current bills and prepare for future financial obligations.

Others give expression to their passion through their hobbies. Jerry takes guys on mountain-climbing trips. Serious climbing—like Mount Everest! Not only does Jerry enjoy the annual trip to base camp at Everest (he hasn't pushed higher—yet), he loves more the chance to speak into the lives of the men who accompany him. That's because Jerry is passionate about developing leaders. He uses these mountain-climbing trips to establish coaching relationships that he invests in the rest of the year—after he finishes his day job as a fund-raising consultant for nonprofit organizations.

Still other people pursue their passion by adopting causes or serving as volunteers on weekends in their communities, schools, churches, or service agencies. Herb builds Habitat houses several weekends a year. Sally spends lots of time working in the community garden she started to produce fresh food for poor urban families. Jane organizes artists' exhibits to raise money to supply AIDS patients with prescription medications. All these people work for a living—but pursuing their passion is where they come alive!

This last group is the one I want to focus on for our discussion. When we talk about serving our neighbors and communities, we often start by thinking about their needs. There is absolutely nothing wrong with this. After all, if I am jumped by a gang and left for dead, I hope someone comes along motivated by my need!

But over time, responding just to need will wear thin. I want to encourage you to build your expression of service around your particular passions or interests. I believe you will be far more motivated, less subject to burnout, and less likely to be easily discouraged. You are far more willing to make the necessary commitments in terms of money, time, and energy when you are fueled by and fueling your passion. You will also be far more contagious in your service—more able to interest others and to draw them into your efforts. Your passion does this. People are drawn to it.

> *Build your expression of service around your particular passions or interests.*

Take Hank Chardos, for instance. He retired from the Internal Revenue Service about a decade ago, but not just so he could play more golf or spend more time with the grandkids. Hank retired early so he could spend more time working with his passion—repairing roofs for poor people who couldn't afford to do it. He started a ministry called Home Works. It grew out of an experience he had on a church mission trip, during which he worked for a week with his daughter to roof a house in a village overseas. Initially the ministry involved just Hank and his own kids. Now, more than a decade later, Home Works has repaired over 1,600 roofs of low-income people through the combined effort of over 20,000 student volunteers (middle school, high school, and college age). These students have learned leadership and construction skills, and have been spiritually instructed and challenged as they've participated in Home Works projects.

I visited one of Hank's work sites during middle school week last summer. About forty middle school students were living in a church's recreation facility for the week—eating, sleeping, and showering there—as a base of operations for the five work projects of the week. They started their day at 6:00 a.m. with prayers and devotions before heading off to their project sites. When they came back together for dinner, they debriefed their experiences of the day. After some relaxation time, they joined together for evening prayers before turning in for the night. In five days they would complete their projects (with the help of adult supervisors and mentors) and then host a banquet in honor of the people they had helped all week.

You want to see passion in action? Hang around Hank. With tears in his eyes, he will tell you about people having a secure roof over their heads for the first time in years. You'll learn of kids who spent a part of several summers of their lives with him, now returning as college students to lead younger volunteers in their efforts. And before long you'll be wanting to help, to give, to figure out a way to be involved.

Hank is a great example of someone allowing their passion to shape their service. And to make a better world. I figure in another twenty years, he will have made amends for all those years persecuting people as an IRS agent!

All across America, millions of us need to turn our passions into service. Including you!

Reflection: What makes your heart beat faster? How could you serve others with this passion?

Talent

Talent matters. It provides a significant clue to your life mission. That's why we'll spend a whole upcoming chapter on helping you figure out what abilities you bring to the table. Unfortunately, many of us are naive about our talents. This is true in part because our culture tends to make sure we all know what we are *not* good at but not necessarily what we *are* good at.

Your best shot at making your best contribution is for you to get better at what you are already good at. We'll talk about how to do this later. For now, just know that your talents are clues to your life becoming more intentional, more meaningful, and more satisfying. What comes easy to you, what you learn to do quickly, what you do that earns you great feedback and gives you personal satisfaction—these are all clues to your talents.

> Your best shot at making your best contribution is for you to get better at what you are already good at.

Doesn't this make sense? If you were created by God for a mission trip to earth, wouldn't he equip you with what you need to accomplish your mission and enjoy it fully? And wouldn't it make sense that he would want you to know what this talent is so you would have an insight into what you have to offer your neighbors?

"I like to start things, to get things going," Ron told me in a coaching session. "I also get bored easily. I don't enjoy getting stuck in a rut or just doing maintenance on existing projects." This self-awareness of talent (Ron has what can be called an "activator strength") has helped him understand his best contribution to others. He is the guy who can be the catalyst to sparkplug people and ideas to begin new initiatives. If you want to get something off the ground or up and running, call Ron. Knowing this keeps Ron looking for fresh ways to serve others. It also keeps him from signing up for an ongoing effort that requires him to do the same thing week after week, month after month.

Paying attention to your talents will help you discover your life mission—and know how to help others with theirs!

Personality

Your personality is your preferred way of engaging the world around you. Unfortunately, when many people think about their personality, the first thoughts that come to their mind are negative. They think about what they don't like about their personality: "I'm too shy, too loud, too [whatever]," or "I'm not engaging, not optimistic, not [whatever]." People who start here never really appreciate what they have going for them. Your personality is not something you have to get over! It's the way you are wired to deal with other people and situations. Learning to appreciate your own personality can actually help you appreciate others' as well.

A young female leader once told me she felt inferior to the rest of the people on the leadership team she served on at her church. As it turned out, the source of her insecurity lay in her concern over her own personality. She was an introvert surrounded by extroverts. She thought that her introversion limited her effectiveness with her team. After I observed her interactions with her peers, I was able to point out to her that it was everyone else who was weird (just kidding). Actually, this young woman had failed to realize how her personal wiring perfectly suited her for the one-on-one mentoring she was providing to young teenage girls as part of her contribution to the ministry. She had no idea that when she said something in a meeting or conversation, the people on her team listened intently. They knew that what she had to say was going to be thought through and thoughtful.

Think about yourself. Are you competitive? That could be a clue that your life mission might involve taking on a cause (or causes) or tackling huge challenges. Do you enjoy helping others succeed? You might be prime material for being a coach or teacher or mentor. Do you have high levels of empathy? (Most of us don't.) You might be a candidate for social work. My point is that your personality offers you great clues to your preferred venues and means of engagement for pursuing your life mission.

Enjoying your life involves building on your personality, not on overcoming it!

Reflection: How does your personality influence the way you want to help others?

_____

_____

_____

Experiences

Your life is not a collection of random encounters, chance happenings, or disconnected occurrences. Your life experiences are a clue to your life mission.

You are living out a story. However, you are only part of the story-making team. You are an important writer for sure, but you are not the main creative talent. God is.

Let's face it. You didn't even get to decide whether or not you were going to show up on the planet, much less when or where. You didn't determine what family you would be a part of, or your ethnicity, or your culture of origin. These decisions were all made for you before you knew anything at all!

Does this mean your life is predetermined? Are you just a puppet on a string? Hardly. Think of it like this. When Cathy and I decided to have children, we already knew that each of our children would have certain experiences. We knew they would have to learn to walk, experience the turmoil of puberty, celebrate love, feel deep disappointment, learn joy, and grow acquainted with sorrow. We knew all this would be a part of their lives, but we did not script how it would come to them. Our girls are very active coconspirators and cowriters in shaping their life stories. Their own choices impact their story-line development significantly. Each is navigating her own unique way through the same issues. Our role as parents has been to support and nurture them into their life's journey.

God does the same for us. Your life has not caught him off guard. He is well aware of the experiences and challenges that have come with your life circumstances. He has been working with your life from a perspective of knowing everything ahead of time. He is the ultimate begin-with-the-end-in-mind guy. Knowing the life challenges you would face, he has dialed into your life what you would need for each chapter. This is why you'll most often see God when you look back across your life experiences. From that perspective, you can more clearly see his intervention and guidance.

For example, a counselor once told me a beautiful story of healing he had witnessed. A woman who had been abused as a child was suffering all kinds of mental disorders. She had been unable to move past her life experiences until one day, under the guidance of this skilled professional, she was able to revisit in her mind a scene from her early life. It was a terrible scene that no child should endure. As the woman recalled and described the incident, she commented that an extra pair of arms was supporting her from behind. The counselor asked her to try to see who those arms belonged to. In her mind's eye, the woman turned and then gasped, "It's Jesus!" In a dramatic way she realized that God had been with her all the time. That realization literally cured the woman's symptoms.

Think back across your own life. Remember those childhood experiences that shaped you. Those school experiences that fired up your imagination. The teacher who took a special interest in you. That first job that maybe taught you what you *didn't* want to do for the rest of your life. Those failures

> *Your life experiences have equipped you to serve others.*

that have actually steered your life in a more rewarding direction. Do you really think these developments were accidental? Of course not. They were ways God was pulling for you. He still is. He is for you, not against you.

Your life experiences have equipped you to serve others. They all have contributed to what you have to offer people. And by serving, you continue to build on these experiences for your own development.

Reflection: What one or two major life experiences have shaped your capacity to help others? How?

_____

_____

_____

The Smile of God

Maybe, like me, you have been profoundly impacted by some movies you've seen. This happened to me in 1981. My wife requested that we go to see a new movie that had been released called *Chariots of Fire*. When I found out it was about an athlete that I had never heard of, my expectations for enjoying it tanked. Boy, was I wrong.

The movie is about two runners competing in the 1924 Olympics. One of those athletes was Eric Liddell, a great Scottish runner. During one scene, he was trying to explain to his sister why he was putting off his departure to China as a missionary to run in the Olympics: "Jenny, God made me for a purpose." Then he hurriedly added, "But he also made me fast. And when I run I feel his pleasure."[5]

That scene was one of those freeze-frame moments for me when time stands still. In just a few seconds, many of my self-calibrations were radically altered. It had never occurred to me that I could bring a smile to the face of God. I didn't even know this truth was taken right out of the Bible: "For the LORD takes delight in his people" (Ps. 149:4). Unfortunately, most of my life to that point had been preoccupied with trying to avoid God's frown of displeasure. I was unaware of how jazzed God is with me. I suddenly realized that I was underenjoying my relationship with God significantly.

I desperately wanted to feel that smile of God. So after the movie was over, I went jogging! It turned out that God wasn't all that happy when I ran. To this day I'm pretty sure he barely tolerates the time I spend on the treadmill. But seriously, doing certain other things in my life gives me a feeling of "Hot dog! This is what I was born for!" And since I believe I was created from the mind and heart of God, I have learned that the rush I am experiencing is indeed his smile. He just loves it when I engage my life mission, since that is his dream for me.

Once I became a father, this truth rang true even more. Thoughts of my children always cause my heart to smile. That was true even in times when, as a parent, I had to correct them in their childhood and youth. My predisposition toward them has remained one of great joy, most especially as I have seen them become the great women I always dreamed they would be, pursuing and engaging their own life missions.

Reflection: When do you feel the smile of God?

———◆———

God delights to see you fulfilled, living your life mission, enjoying abundant life. After all, that's what he's had in mind for you all along!

So get off your donkey and help somebody. They need it—and you've got a lot of living to do!

5

THE BIG REVEAL

The deal lumbered toward completion. The papers were ready to sign. All of the negotiations between Roger and his potential new employer had gone smoothly. The salary and perks package, along with the major job responsibilities, had all been hashed out with the human resources director.

Then came an unexpected email from his supervisor-to-be, fleshing out the expectations of how Roger would actually carry out his duties. The gap between the stated expectations and the real ones was significant. Roger suddenly realized that to do the job the way the new boss expected was going to require twice the time away from home than he had counted on. One of the reasons Roger had even begun the job search was to get away from the travel time required by his current job. Now here he was looking at it all over again.

Roger picked up the phone and called his new boss to explore the possibility of reducing the travel requirements. A brief conversation confirmed that the expectations communicated in the email were nonnegotiable. Roger hung up the phone, sighed as he looked down at the papers, then picked up his pen and signed his life away. . . .

The guy seated next to me on the transcontinental flight animatedly talked to me about his work, his wife, his child, his travel abroad, and his political views. The flight attendant interrupted our conversation to hand him a glass of wine. "Compliments of the lady in 9C," he said to the startled passenger. I was then treated to an explanation by my seatmate. The lady, he explained as he sipped his wine, was someone he had met in the airport while waiting for the flight to board. Casual conversation had turned into lunch together and a few drinks. "She's nice-looking," he said as he unfastened his seat belt and headed up the aisle. He spent the rest of the flight hovering around 9C. . . .

"I lost my job last week," Cassie told the class during the opening introductions of a two-week doctoral seminar I was teaching. "I'm an accountant. I've been under pressure to cook the books at the company I work for to show a better year-end performance than what's real. I've never made a misleading entry in twenty years of accounting, and I'm not going to start now. I will not be unethical."

Three different people in three different situations facing three different sets of choices. One common denominator: their choices revealed their personal values.

What's the Big Deal?

You may have developed the personal mission we talked about in the last chapter. However, unless you have the values to support this vision, it will remain an illusory dream. You don't want that to happen. You want to figure out what really drives you, what your core values are, so that your personal mission in life can be fully realized.

Values are beliefs in action. They shape our decisions, determine how we spend our time and money, and play into how we conduct our relationships with others. They are not just what we say are the most important things to us; our real values are what we live out in our day-to-day lives. Our values are more than preferences. They are the things we hold most dear—so dear, in fact, that we live according to them, whether or not we realize it. Respect, integrity, trust, healthy relationships, travel, fun, leisure, work, acquisition, adventure, image, service, security, financial gain, faith, family, loyalty, health, comfort, risk—these are only a few of the values that frequently show up in our lists of what is important to us.

> Our values are more than preferences. They are the things we hold most dear— so dear, in fact, that we live according to them, whether or not we realize it.

In seminars and in coaching sessions, when I ask people to identify their core values, they often have trouble coming up with their lists. That's when I suggest they go home and ask their spouses what their core values are. Or I tell them to ask their co-workers to give them feedback. "They can list them for you in an instant," I tell them. That's because the people in our lives experience our values all the time. Our co-workers, friends, family members, and, yes, the people we serve—anyone who spends significant time with us—can tell us what is *really* important to us. Just ask them!

Your Values Are Showing

Your values, whatever they are, are coming across loud and clear to your neighbors.

Values play into your service to others in a couple of important ways. First, as you engage people and their life circumstances, you'll often find your own life values challenged by what you encounter. Second, you communicate your personal values in your interactions with people, especially those you serve.

Let me illustrate both points with my friend Sally's experience. When I met her, Sally was a first-year social worker in a county hospital, fresh out of graduate school with her master's degree in social work. Dealing with the dark underbelly of our culture every day was proving to be an eye-opening and challenging education beyond the classroom. "I'm really having to rethink my attitudes toward poverty and people affected by it," she told me. She went on to say that her beliefs had always been shaped by a strong sense of personal responsibility. "I pretty much thought people who are poor had made that choice. Now I realize how much the deck is stacked against so many people." This shift of values was not just a political and economic one for this young woman. It was, in fact, changing long-held convictions, even prejudices. Becoming acquainted with people's real life-and-death struggles was changing *her*.

Now three years into her work, Sally admits that she has become more empathetic toward those in need, but she is also frustrated by the choices they make. "They keep choosing a course of action that guarantees nothing will change for the better for them," she recently observed with a sigh. "I can't help them if that's the case."

Sally's strong value of personal responsibility is reasserting itself as she recalibrates her long-held belief with the reality of institutional poverty in our nation. This value flavors her interactions with her clients every day. While Sally has significantly increased her display of empathy for the people she serves, she also presents to them the consequences of the choices they make. Sally, in effect, is sharing her own values in every one of these interactions.

As Sally's case points out, our values are showing! They are behaviorally revealed. Just saying something is important to us doesn't make it so. What we *do* is what we believe. The rest is just wishful thinking, self-deception, or mere parroting of something that someone told us should be valuable to us.

Do you see how important our core values are in our dealings with other people? The priest and Levite in the story of the Good Samaritan honored their core values by passing by the beat-up victim. The Samaritan also acted out his values by stopping to help. His values propelled him off his donkey.

> *Just saying something is important to us doesn't make it so. What we **do** is what we believe.*

Reflection: What do you think are your top five core values?

_____

_____

_____

Where Did You Pick Up Your Values?

By now you're beginning to see just how powerful your personal core values are in shaping your life experiences. This realization may have you wondering, "Where did I get these values?"

You aren't born with your values. They're not genetic. They are selected and shaped by years of choices, some of which you were making before you were even aware that you were building your values set.

When you understand where you picked up your values, you are better able to evaluate them. This is especially important information if you want to change or shift your values, or even discard some.

We get our values from a variety of influences. Authority figures—like parents, coaches, and teachers—play an important role, especially early on. Our faith traditions also typically weigh in as a significant force in our values formation. Culture is another major player in this process. We breathe culture like fish breathe water. Flowing around and through us, culture saturates us with whatever is in the "water," which itself has been influenced by media, politics, economics, and major events. Friends and co-workers also contribute to our values. All these influences combine with our major life events and experiences to produce in us a set of values.

A couple of stories can help you see what I'm talking about. In each of these accounts, you will see a variety of values-shaping factors in play.

My mom grew up with an alcoholic father. This meant she became an adult child of an alcoholic. I didn't know what that was until I was in my late thirties and could begin to understand the negative impact of some key life lessons that she had learned from her experience and had then passed on to me. ACAs (Adult Children of Alcoholics) learn three significant lessons: don't trust (don't let others in), don't feel (especially problem emotions, like anger), and don't tell (shame). If you were parented by someone with those core convictions, I don't have to tell you how powerful they are in shaping your childhood and even adult experiences. For me, these values were ingredients for a wicked brew of burnout in my late thirties. That experience actually served as the catalyst for me to sort out my values and where I got them.

A friend of mine recently shared with a group of us a part of his life story that none of us knew. We had only known him as a successful attorney, a senior partner of a large law firm. Stephen graduated from a prestigious private college Phi Beta Kappa and graduated first in his law class. What we didn't know until he told us was that he could not read until he was in third grade! Up until then he was considered "slow." But a third-grade teacher refused that diagnosis and saw a spark of intelligence in him that she fanned into flame. "It was that teacher who helped me believe I was smart," Stephen said.

That early-life experience created a soft spot in this very aggressive and competitive lawyer for people who he feels have not been given a chance or have been overlooked. This in turn has influenced the causes he champions and his engagement with various

> *Your values shape your character. Your character shapes your choices. Your choices shape your life.*

charities and neighbor-helping activities. These are values-based decisions all influenced by that third-grade teacher's impact on his life.

Your values shape your character. Your character shapes your choices. Your choices shape your life. That's why it is so important to know where you picked up the values you carry with you in your life backpack.

Reflection: Who packed the backpack of your life values?

_____

_____

_____

Are You Stuck with Your Values?

By now you may be wondering, are you saddled with the values you currently have adopted? The answer is "yes" if you haven't taken the time to figure out what your values are and where you got them. In this case the autopilot values you have are running your life show and you feel powerless to change the story line. People unaware of their values frequently don't understand how their behaviors are sabotaging their lives. So they are bound to keep revisiting the same scenarios over and over. Not good.

The good news is that you are *not* stuck with your current values set. Once you know what they are and where you got them, you can decide whether or not to keep them.

For instance, once I knew how and where I had picked up certain values from my family of origin (don't trust, don't feel, don't tell), I could make conscious decisions about which values I wanted to keep and which ones I wanted to discard. I was no longer destined to respond to forces I didn't understand. I decided that I did not want to shut people out of my life by failing to trust others. I formed a small group of guys who helped me work through some of my issues. I made friends with a counselor who could speak into my life. I began to try to articulate my emotions rather than stuffing them (my wife had to help me learn to ride this bike).

Resetting the defaults of my values has proven challenging. There have been plenty of occasions where I have slipped back to my old thinking and behaviors. But overall I can see progress. One thing is certain, however: not changing my values was going to keep me on the path to a place where I visited but didn't want to live!

> *A fundamental shift has to occur in* **you** *if your community is to be a better place.*

Maybe you too have decided to change some of your values. The changes you want to make may have nothing to do with the subject of this book. On the other hand, maybe they do. Perhaps you haven't loved your neighbor as yourself, but you want to. You realize that some of your values (like security or comfort) have kept you from genuinely and generously meeting the needs of those in your community who need your help. So now you've decided to do something about it. And you realize that a fundamental shift has to occur in *you* if your community is to be a better place.

How Do You Change Your Values?

Changing values isn't easy. But it can be done! Every day people are undergoing life transformations all around us. Addicts are kicking their habits. People are experiencing profound spiritual encounters. Formerly self-absorbed and selfish people are beginning to live their lives for the benefit of others who need their assistance. All these examples prove that you can change your values.

You have already made the first step those people had to make. You have moved from what some psychologists call the precontemplation and contemplation stage (where you aren't ready to make significant change) to a point where you are considering what next to do. Congratulations! This first step is essential to everything that follows. You now need to take three additional steps.

Clarify Your Values Gap

Shift your values to be ruthlessly honest about your current values set. People engaged in recovery say it something like this: conduct a fierce moral inventory of your life. No holds barred. No denial. No hiding or wishful thinking. Just the truth.

At a few points in this chapter, I have given some questions to tease out your values. You might want to go back over them. This process is called values clarification. You may not like what you have found out, but until you face the truth of what really drives you, there is little chance for change.

Get other people involved in this process. They should be those who have the closest view of you—your spouse, your children, the people you work with, even your friends. These people will have the perspective you need. Ask them what they think your values are. This can be painful but fun at the same time—that is up to you.

Most important, bring your real life to this process. Review your calendar, your checkbook, your friendships, your hobbies, your family relationships, your habits and patterns—all in search of what's really important to you. How you are spending your time, money, and energy are clear tips-offs to the values that are driving your life ship. Don't settle for answers that fall short of the real truth about you.

Reflection: When will you begin this values assessment? Who will be involved with you in doing it?

_____

_____

_____

Practice Your Values

Another important step in shifting values is to act them out. A fancy way of saying this is that you need to create venues where you can practice the new values you want to have. Remember, values show up in our behavior.

I have already mentioned that I frequently speak in church gatherings. Most of the time, I address the need for God's people to be people of blessing, a subject we have already talked about. I then help them think whom they can bless intentionally—hospitality workers in restaurants, co-workers, people they meet in chance encounters, whomever. Usually I give them a phrase they can use: "How can I ask God to bless you?" This question picks up on both aspects of the covenant of being the people of God—that he is a blessing God and it is our job to make sure people know that about him. I conclude by encouraging God's people to watch for him to show up and show off in these encounters.

Just this week a pastor forwarded an email sent in from someone who was part of a recent gathering where I spoke on these themes. The subject line of the email read, "Our homework about praying for God to bless." Here's the story:

> I was driving home from work and frantically calling people about this big event on Wednesday night. . . . I was calling Ben and got one number off. So I called the wrong number. The lady was really nice and was even laughing about it. I asked her, "How can I ask God to bless you?" She sighed hard, and we had a fifteen-minute conversation as she shared that she and her son-in-law both need jobs, and her daughter and this same son-in-law are expecting twins (they live with her). It was easy for me to recommend a website I know that contains awesome job possibilities for both of them. She called me back later last night and asked, "Is this my wrong number friend?" Then she said that she and her son-in-law looked at the site and between them found and applied for fourteen jobs. She said, "There are NO wrong numbers." I told her I was just glad that she let God show up and show off.

The "homework" assignment did what it was designed to do! It provided a way for this person to practice a different value. I predict that this way of living will be so much fun that it will become more routine for this person.

How about you? What venues can you create to practice the values you want to keep? Presumably being a good neighbor to those in need is one of those values. Figure out what you want to do and schedule time to do it. Join a service organization or determine to do three acts of kindness every day. Volunteer at some local charity.

You get the picture. Make deliberate, intentional choices to fund your values with time, money, and energy. The actions you need to take may range from doing something different for thirty minutes a day to doing something different for the rest of your life. Unless you take this step of figuring out how you are going to practice your values—how you are going to live them out in specific action—you will simply be doing more wishful thinking.

Reflection: What new behaviors do you need to practice? How will you "fund" them (time, money, etc.)?

Be Accountable

All my life I have been on a diet. Kind of. I've lost hundreds of pounds—okay, the same pounds hundreds of times. Sometimes for weeks and months I talk about my need to lose weight. But only the day when I step on the scale do I mean business. At that point I am willing to be accountable.

No significant life change happens without accountability. So write out your values and how you plan to live them out. Share these with your family, trusted friends, and spiritual guides who will coach you and encourage you to maintain these values in your life.

We all know that doing things together with others strengthens our resolve. This is why Alcoholics Anonymous (AA), Weight Watchers, and a host of other groups aimed at life and behavioral transformation, including those helping people break the poverty cycle, all insist on group involvement. Finding others who can participate with you and encourage you will raise not only your accountability but probably your chances of success in the values-change process.

A lot of times we think of accountability in negative terms—like empowering someone to slap our hands when we misbehave. I prefer to think of accountability partners as cheerleaders who are pulling for you and coaches who celebrate your progress and victories. Establishing accountability partners with this mind-set allows you to build a support team for making desired changes. It will also create an environment that encourages your individual efforts.

> *Finding others who can participate with you and encourage you will raise not only your accountability but probably your chances of success in the values-change process.*

Here's a group experience to prove what I mean. It's excerpted from an email account forwarded to me by a pastor. It involves three people who were part of a congregational gathering where I delivered my usual message. They went out to eat right after the worship service.

As we got to the restaurant, we remarked that we had to find a fourth person to share our Groupon. No worries, we would look for someone eating alone and pick up their lunch. Well, Matt found someone eating by himself, went to talk with him regarding our Groupon, and offered the man a free lunch. The man turned him down! Daniel and I couldn't believe it. Matt thinks the gentleman did not understand how he explained it.

We continued to eat and later noticed a woman sitting by herself. The guys said it was my turn, so I approached the woman and asked if she was dining alone. She said she was, and I explained that I would like to buy her lunch as the second half of my Groupon deal. She said, "I knew God sent me here for a reason today. I accept your blessing." . . .

Later, when I was in line to pay, the lady approached me and said. "I feel like there is something more going on here than just your buying my lunch." I then asked her if there was anything I could pray for her about. She said yes. Her mother-in-law was ill and could use my prayers. She said her husband would normally be eating with her, but he was in Ohio with his mother. I told her I would definitely pray for her and tell others to as well. She was grateful and gracious as I continued to check out.

I was stunned! I am an emotional person anyway, but I kept it together long enough to exit the restaurant to meet the guys. I then told them what had taken place while in line. Both were so excited and agreed to pray for the mother-in-law as well.

Every person in this lunchtime group was encouraged by the others, each taking their turn at being a person of blessing and then celebrating the results. I bet when this got shared in their next church service, it encouraged some others to step up their own intention to be a person of blessing.

Reflection: Who are you going to include in your team of values accountability partners? How will you make yourself accountable to them?

_____

_____

_____

It's Your Turn

Recently I had dinner with a young church-planting couple. They told me the fantastic story of how their new congregation had made a significant change in ministry. By holding an outdoor worship service in a park, they had met some homeless people there and developed a meaningful ministry to them in the ensuing weeks and months.

This development led to an unexpected turn of events. The new congregation is located in an upscale part of the city, and most of the constituents are from nearby neighborhoods. The inclusion of homeless in every church activity, including worship and fellowship functions, had created some cultural tension as two very disparate parts of society were being thrown together in a new way.

This young couple, determined to be people of blessing, made a smart decision to bring the issue out into the open. At a church leadership meeting, the pastor asked for people to voice their concerns and observations.

After several people spoke about various issues, one woman stood to address the group. This person is a well-known philanthropist in the city, as well as being politically connected. In other words, she is a leading citizen of that community. With measured emotion and genteel humility, she said, "You all know of my involvement in lots of charitable work in our city. I serve on boards, write checks, and make policy decisions that determine how service is provided to many people. I have always thought of how I was changing the lives of people on the receiving end of those decisions. But the last few months, through our homeless ministry, I have become personally involved with some very needy people. And I have made a discovery: they are changing me!"

> *Your decision whether or not to help others also reveals whether or not you want to be better yourself.*

The call to imitate the Good Samaritan challenges you to cultivate values that move you off your donkey. Your decision whether or not to help others also reveals whether or not you want to be better yourself.

It's your donkey on the line.

6

TAKE YOUR BEST SHOT

Your best shot at making your best contribution to the world is for you to get better at what you are already good at. When you come to a greater awareness of your strengths and begin to develop them, you become more of the person you were designed by God to be. In addition, the quality of the contribution you make to others can exponentially increase. It's never too late to start building on your strengths. And it's never too early to start building on your strengths.

I am indebted to the late Don Clifton, former CEO of The Gallup Organization, for shaping many of my thoughts about building on our strengths. His two books, *Soar with Your Strengths* and *Now, Discover Your Strengths*, provide a philosophical framework along with practical suggestions for identifying and building on strengths. Don used to say, among lots of other words of wisdom, "God didn't make people to get work done; he made work to get people done." His commitment to developing people still inspires me.

In this chapter we'll take a look at how you can determine what you are good at, along with strategies to help you do those things more. Your life will be more productive, fun, and energizing. The people around you will be blessed by your talents. Both you and they will be better. That's the point.

Talents, Competencies, and Strengths

By *talent* I mean the raw abilities and aptitudes you possess, like speed, intelligence, musicality, athleticism, artistic sense, intuition, ability to connect with other people—the list goes on and on. You don't create your talents. You are gifted with them. But you can develop them.

Added to talent are your competencies. These are specific skills or skill sets, such as technological ability, administrative ability, good communication skills in speaking or writing, team-building skills, sewing and cooking skills—again the list is as endless as people's activities. Competencies are learned behaviors that build on the foundation of talent.

Talents and competencies intersect to create potential strength sets. For instance, a person with musical talent has many different options as to how and where that talent will play out. Some musically talented people perform while others teach; some write music while others conduct. Likewise, skills can be at the service of many talents. For instance, technological prowess can be employed by musicians, artists, writers, interior designers, tool makers, and carpenters.

Every human being is talented and possesses abilities of some sort. The presence of talents and competencies in and of themselves, however, does not constitute a realized strength. These abilities turn into strengths only when they are identified and practiced through life experience—when they are employed. In other words, strengths emerge with the intentional application of these abilities to life challenges in various arenas—home, work, school, hobbies, and so on.

The more aware of this process you become, the more able you are to intentionally build on your strengths.

The strength-building process does not automatically take place in people's lives. Some people have undiscovered talents. Others fail to identify and cultivate the skills necessary to enhance their talents. Many people squander their skills by applying them to talents they don't actually possess. Bottom line: lots of people do not know what they are good at. Many more have underdeveloped strengths. In both cases people and our communities are cheated out of their talents and kept from becoming all they could be.

> *You need to know what you bring to the table and figure out how to get better at it.*

For you to engage life fully, you need to know what you bring to the table and figure out how to get better at it.

Talent Matters

Developing a strengths approach to life begins with a clear and honest assessment of your talents.

I would love to be a guard on a professional basketball team. I see myself flying up and down the basketball court, developing plays, passing the ball at just the right moment to a team member breaking for the basket, or pulling up out of a dead run to sink a three-pointer—wait a minute, I'm dreaming! It's never going to happen! I could go to NBA guard school, be mentored by an NBA guard, and join an NBA guard learning cluster. None of it would matter. It would be a waste of time and very frustrating, both for me and for the unfortunate players going through the experience with me.

I will never be an NBA guard. Not because of a lack of passion or a failure to dream or the reluctance to believe I can. It's because I don't have the talent for it. Period. My time and energies will be far better spent in working on something I do well so I can do it better.

The same thing is true for you. The beginning point to building on your strengths is to know what your talents and skills are. But there's the rub. Many of you are naive about your strengths. You simply don't know what they are.

There can be many reasons why you might lack awareness of your strengths. Sometimes this inadequate self-knowledge results from not having explored your talents adequately. Perhaps you were not encouraged to try out your talents as a kid. Maybe your parents or teachers or coaches were more interested in shaping your performance in areas of non-strength.

Maybe you bought into what I call the "balance myth." People certainly are not balanced. Talent is not equally distributed. In the area of your talents, you are severely out of round! You stick out like a sore thumb. You are a standard deviation or two ahead of the pack. Whatever analogy you use, the point is that you have something others don't have—and vice versa. If you bought into the balance myth, you may still be trying to be "well-rounded," which means you probably never focused enough on your actual talents to develop them fully. As a result, you still may not know what you really can do well.

Perhaps another reason you may not know what you are good at is that you have taken your talents for granted. This calls out another myth that goes like this: "Only what comes hard counts." In other words, you may think that things that come easy to you don't count as talents because you didn't work hard for them.

Here's the truth: when it comes to talent, it comes easy! You don't work for your talents. You were given them by God. If you don't understand this truth and believe instead that *you* have to produce your talents, you likely will find yourself at odds with your design parameters.

Please don't hear what I am *not* saying. I am not urging you to do only the things in life that come easy. You certainly need to be industrious and responsible and committed to discipline. Much of life requires lots of effort. The trash doesn't carry itself out, and dishes don't wash themselves. However, if you believe the myth that it only counts if it comes hard, you may miss discovering your genuine talents. You will likely undervalue them or dismiss them because you didn't *earn* them. You might not even recognize them as talents at all!

For example, Ted Williams, legendary baseball hitter, was reputedly heard giving some advice to a young player who was facing and fanning at ninety-five-mile-per-hour fastballs. "Just watch the stitches," he suggested.

"What stitches?" the rookie asked.

"On the baseball!" Williams responded. Then he reportedly launched into a discourse on how the rotation of the stitches on the baseball influenced its behavior between the pitching mound and home plate.

"You can see stitches?!" the young player exclaimed.

What Ted Williams did not know was that, for most people, a fastball at ninety-five miles per hour starts out as a blur and then disappears on its sixty-foot-six-inch journey from the pitching mound to home plate. When asked what else he could see, Williams said he could sometimes read the commissioner's signature on the ball. Incredible!

Williams dispensed well-meaning but poor advice when he admonished the rookie to "watch the stitches." He thought everyone could see the stitches. Eventually it was discovered that the baseball legend had 20/10 vision. What came easily to Ted Williams because of his eyesight didn't come to other people at all! No matter how badly you want 20/10 vision, you can't practice yourself into it. You either have it or you don't.

That's the way it is with talent. You either have it or you don't. It's a gift you didn't earn. You just received it as part of who you were created to be.

You see "stitches" in some way. Just reflect on where and how you are amazed (even sometimes annoyed) that other people seem to struggle with something that comes easy to you. You may have thought that they weren't concentrating or trying hard enough. You might even have decided that they were lazy or uninterested or just wanting to aggravate you! Your stitch-seeing ability isn't a fair standard to apply to them.

The fact that you don't get to decide on your talents may not sit well with you. You may prefer to believe you can decide what abilities you will have through self-determination. Part of developing a strengths approach to life is to come to grips with and be at peace with the talents you have been given, not to agitate and exhaust yourself trying to obtain gifts that are not marked out for you. Learning to be content with what abilities you do have plays a huge role in acknowledging God in your life.

> *Part of developing a strengths approach to life is to come to grips with and be at peace with the talents you have been given, not to agitate and exhaust yourself trying to obtain gifts that are not marked out for you.*

One of Jesus's famous stories is frequently called the parable of the talents (see Matt. 25:14–30). In the parable, the word *talents* refers to money (that's what some coins were called in those days). Servants each received a different amount of money to work with. This money came from their master, who made the decision about who got what. The expectation of the master was that each servant would try to build on the talents he received. Two of the three did so and earned not only their master's approval but greater investment opportunities. The third servant did not try to grow his talent. Instead he dug a hole and hid it. He earned a sharp rebuke from his master and had his money taken away. Through this story Jesus teaches clearly that the avenue to abundant living lies in talent (strength) development.

Nowhere in Scripture are we told we are going to be held responsible for developing talents we don't have. This is another reason not to waste our efforts focusing on nonexistent talents. Yet we *are* told (in the parable of the talents and others) that we are going to be held accountable for talents that we do have.

God's expectation is that we will work with what we have been given, to expand and develop it further. Why? Is it because he is a difficult taskmaster who is hard to please? No, though he does have the right not to like it when people squander his gifts. The truth is, God knows that we enjoy life more when we are working with what he gave us for this life. And he has given us our talents with the clear intention that we share them with others. Knowing and using our talents is a clear way we will be people of blessing to those around us.

Reflection: Where do you see "stitches"?

_____

_____

_____

Name Those Strengths

You are probably asking yourself a few questions by now: *What are my talents? How can I know that my hunches about what I'm good at are on target?* Maybe you are even a little nervous about this investigation. You want to make sure you don't miss the boat at this point or spend all your life barking up the wrong talent tree.

There's good news: you can know what your strengths are! God has not left you without substantial clues as to what strengths he has dialed into you. These clues are not buried or hidden—they are in plain sight, woven into your life experience.

Clue: What Interests You?

A good place to begin your strength-awareness process is to start with those things that get your attention pretty easily. These can be causes, hobbies, special interests, passions, even unfulfilled yearnings that won't go away. The arenas for these interests can range from family life to business pursuits to spiritual passions to community involvement to leisure activity.

You should consider the following questions: What situations, challenges, assignments are you drawn to? Why are you drawn to them? Why do you enjoy doing them so much? What skills do you use when you do them? What part of these activities brings you the greatest satisfaction? How do others respond to your efforts in these areas?

Lyle considered some of these questions when he faced a fork-in-the-road experience brought on by a midcareer shift in work. Translation: the company he worked for was bought out and his job was phased out. With a few months' severance in the bank, he had some time to consider his next move. As he and I chatted about his situation, the conversation drifted toward Lyle's obvious passion: helping young teenage boys make the transition into manhood. From his own background of struggles—among them being that he had grown up without a father—he had developed a heart to be there for boys at a critical passage in their lives. When we met, Lyle was already helping out with the community boys' club and coaching Upward basketball, a popular community recreational program used by many churches.

As Lyle thought through his passion, using some of the questions listed above, his strengths just popped out. He

110

realized he possessed a lot of empathy—an ingredient that many people don't have—combined with a skill set that made him a great developer of people and a natural coach for basketball and for life. Lyle determined to seek the most productive environment where he could exercise his passion and talents in helping young men make the transition from adolescence to manhood.

This fresh awareness of his strengths led Lyle to seek employment in a youth outreach program sponsored by a well-known service group. "I don't want to spend the rest of my life just waiting for five o'clock to come so I can do what I really want to do," he said. Even though the pay is substantially less than that of his old job, Lyle's zest for life has gone way up. He is operating out of his strengths!

Reflection: What interests you?

Clue: What Brings You Fulfillment?

Lyle's evaluation of his strengths uncovered a significant clue that many others have also found to help them in their own strengths discovery: figuring out what gives them a sense of personal fulfillment. This is frequently linked to those things in our lives that provide us with joy and a sense of significance. These feelings are not just about the activity itself; they usually uncover what the activity signifies or means to us—why we find fulfillment when we are engaged with it.

Remember Eric Liddell's explanation to his sister in *Chariots of Fire* about why he was pursuing his dream of running in the 1924 Olympics? "When I run, I feel his [God's] pleasure."

For Liddell, the very act of running was an act of luxurious self-fulfillment. He enjoyed a deep and profound spiritual connectedness in his soul when he celebrated his talent.

You see, your strengths are also your needs. You were designed to flex your strengths. If you don't get to practice what you're good at, you are underdeveloped as a person. Your soul is undernourished. Your time and energy are being spent on pursuits that don't allow you to feel the smile of God.

> *Your strengths are also your needs. You were designed to flex your strengths.*

While I have never felt God's pleasure when jogging, there are other activities that do jazz me. I just love it when a person or group of people gets a fresh perspective that literally changes the way they are going about life. When God graces me by allowing me to be a catalytic part of that experience, I am flooded with a deep sense of fulfillment and well-being.

Reflection: Think of what you do that makes you feel, *This is what I was born to do!* What talents are you using in that particular activity? How can you reorder your life so you can do more of what brings you fulfillment?

_____

_____

_____

Clue: What Do You Do Well?

Eric Liddell's declaration to his sister would have been much less profound if he had not been a good runner. However, because of his obvious talent, his conviction carried great weight.

In the search for talent, you should ask yourself what you are really good at. The fact that you enjoy doing something doesn't qualify it as a strength unless you actually bring ability to it. It might qualify as a hobby or diversion but not as a strength. I enjoy playing golf—every five years or so—but no one on the course with me would mistake golf as a talent of mine.

A good place to start this investigation is with other people's feedback. Pay attention to what others have told you about what you do well. They may help you discover hidden talents or affirm the suspicions you already have about what you do well. What is the earliest compliment you can remember about something you did? What have people through the years told you that you do well? What have you received positive feedback on in terms of your performance in the past few weeks? What patterns do you see in this feedback? What combinations of talents have impressed others?

If you reflect on these questions, you will at least have a beginning set of talents that others have affirmed in you. Keep in mind this may not (and probably won't) reflect all of your talents since most people don't get to see all of your good stuff. However, you will gain insight into some of your outstanding abilities to work with in developing your strengths.

You might find yourself struggling with this part of the talent investigation for one or both of two reasons. First, you may lack people in your life who are affirming and positive in their feedback disposition. Unfortunately, I find this situation far too often. While involved with a collegiate leadership initiative some years ago, I conducted a strengths workshop. During a break, a college student poured out her heart to me. Between sobs she recounted a painful history of being put down all her life, especially by her family, for the very things she had just learned in the workshop were true talents of hers! The Gallup StrengthsFinder, a well-known instrument to help people identify and build on their talents, had identified her as a future-oriented person with a high capacity for vision. Yet this had never been appreciated by the people around her. "Get your head out of the clouds!" and "Plant your feet on the ground!" were two phrases that had been thrown at her all her life. Consequently, over the years this young woman had begun to doubt herself, wondering if something was wrong with her. As you can imagine, the discovery that "futuristic" is a talent was incredibly freeing and affirming for her.

A second reason you might struggle with other people's feedback has nothing to do with the information. Instead, it involves something about you. Maybe you have the propensity to focus on negative feedback rather than on positive affirmation. Some people (maybe you!) can hear one hundred compliments accompanied by one piece of criticism—and they obsess over the one negative comment! This way of thinking explains, in part, why some people spend their energies trying to plug all the gaps or deficiencies in their abilities rather than building on their strengths. They have unwittingly handed over to their critics and negative voices the primary power in shaping them. What a pity! All of us have talent deficits—things we are not too good at. Don't let criticism of these areas hinder you from finding out what you *are* good at.

> Some people spend their energies trying to plug all the gaps or deficiencies in their abilities rather than building on their strengths.

In addition to your own life experience review, you also have available to you resources that can give objective feedback of and assess your talents and strengths. Local colleges and universities, career counseling centers, and even some employment agencies frequently provide some instruments you can use to gain greater insight into what you are good at.

As I mentioned, the coaching instrument for strengths assessment and development that I use a lot is the Gallup StrengthsFinder, developed by Don Clifton and the research scientists at Gallup. Don's greatest passion was to help people grow into their strengths. His work has helped to spark the whole strengths revolution. Because he was completely committed to harnessing his own talent in pursuit of his dream, tens of thousands of people have been set free to do the same.

Reflection: What have people or instruments told you that you are good at?

Clue: What Comes Quick and Easy to You?

Not only does talent come easy (a truth we have already discussed), it comes quick! In those skills where you excel, your learning curve is fairly easily mastered, certainly in comparison to learning in areas of non-talent.

This insight can also help you determine where you probably should *not* spend your energy. I have to settle for functionality in the digital world. The ability to interface with the technology just doesn't come easy. This is a huge clue for my career field. No one who has worked with me would ever expect me to be a candidate for the technology help desk.

As obvious as this truth seems, however, I keep running into college kids who are majoring in accounting or law or whatever, even though every single skill they gain in that field results only from major effort on their part. Often they are trying to please a parent or hate to admit that they made a mistake in choosing a career path. I have seen some of these young adults get a whole new outlook on life simply by changing to a field where they actually get it—quick and easy!

When my older daughter was in high school, she struggled in her honors math classes. And I couldn't help her. I don't know a parabola from a paramecium. One night I suggested to her that she consider dropping down one level in her studies, which would still leave her in advanced math but not in the same class with the math geniuses. "Look," I told her, "you and I both know you aren't going into a career that relies on your math abilities. Spending hours on this stuff every night is just taking time away from the studies that *are* going to power your job opportunities."

She is a high achiever, so it was difficult for her to make the change, but she followed my advice. The results were immediate in terms of emotional and psychological relief (I'm talking about my own since I no longer had to face my math limitations every night). Today she is a highly functioning young professional building a great career around her strengths.

Prior to my conversion to a strengths philosophy (thank you, Don Clifton), I would never have made that suggestion to my daughter. Instead, I would have said something like, "You started the class, you are going to finish it!" or "You just need to work harder at it," or some other equally brilliant advice.

Again, I'm not talking about character-building situations. I'm talking about competency issues. You are going to be much happier cooperating with God in how he made you! And, by the way, these competencies are also clues to how you can best help other people.

So, for the sake of your neighbor as well as yourself, figure out what you are good at!

Reflection: What can you do almost without effort? What do you learn quickly?

_____

_____

_____

Lower Your "Rent"

When people realize they are paying too much rent for their living space, they make a move to lower their rent. You might need to take the same approach in creating more margins for exercising your strengths.

We all pay some "rent" to get to do the things we want to. However, many people are paying too high a price. If that's you, figure out a way to quit doing stuff that brings you no energy or that you're not particularly good at so you have the time and energy to use your talents more. Not only will you be more productive, you will be a happier person—and so will the people around you!

> Figure out a way to quit doing stuff that brings you no energy or that you're not particularly good at so you have the time and energy to use your talents more.

Some people feel they have no choice but to experience the smile of God only occasionally. How sad! How untrue! Why would God let you get a look at your strengths only to say, "Uh-uh-uh, not too much of that now!" That sounds like the devil to me!

Here is where some strategy on your part certainly is called for, as well as possibly some sacrificing. Truth is, many of us blame other people for the steep rent payments we are making

117

when we can make the decision ourselves to move to a lower rent environment. Here are some moves you can initiate or strategies you might pursue.

Revamp Your Job Description(s)

While I obviously have your workplace in mind, you are actually working jobs in lots of arenas—at home, at your service club, at church, wherever you have responsibility. Why not rethink your duties and how you want to get them done? Propose to your supervisor, your partner, your team members, or your spouse how you would like to reapportion your duties to fit your strengths. You can also suggest some alternative ways of accomplishing your various assignments using more of your strengths.

While serving in a leadership capacity of a not-for-profit institution, I had partial responsibility for implementing a strengths philosophy, including shaping the employee annual review into a strengths coaching session. Most of the interview between supervisors and those who reported to them involved figuring out how to remove obstacles that got in the way of strength development as well as figuring out ways that unused strengths could find expression.

One team rewrote all their job descriptions to fit their team members' individual strengths. They listed all the jobs that had to be accomplished, then figured out who should have each assignment. Sometimes tasks were broken into various components so that a team of people worked together to pull it off. Even the office space was reallocated, and a person who was more energized by personal interaction moved into the receptionist role and office space. This move provided enormous relief to the employee who previously occupied that spot and favored a much less interrupted work pattern.

You might be thinking, *This will never fly at my office—or house.* Truthfully, most of us have more leverage to do this than we think. This is especially true if you are considered a valued member of the team (hopefully your spouse sees you this way!). Take initiative and responsibility here. Don't just complain. Offer solutions and a trial-run period. Don't just present a problem; be part of a solution.

Outsource the Stuff You Don't Do Well

Think through this in every arena. Perhaps you can pay for some household help or spend part of your office budget on outsourced assistance. If you can't afford to outsource completely, consider swapping your talents with someone else's—help them out if they'll help you out. Both of you benefit. Call in some help from your fellow workers.

This is exactly what Diane did. While she was good at project management, she was less talented at project design. So she consulted with others in her office, receiving and delivering quality help that raised everyone's performance on the team.

Recruit Other People to Partner with You

Make the swapping-off strategy we just talked about more permanent. Make a deal at home or the office. Exchange some of your assignments and responsibilities for ones that match your strengths better.

For instance, Tom had the notion that it was his job to handle the money at his house. His dad had done this in his family of origin, so he thought it was part of being a man and husband. The problem was, Tom couldn't handle money all that well. Besides hating math, he was too impulsive to stay within a budget. Even though he wanted to excel at household finances, it just wasn't in his strength set. His wife, on the other hand, was very capable in that area. It was a great day when Tom relinquished control of the checkbook to his

119

wife. Then he took on some other household duties that freed up his wife up to take over the finances. Their marriage partnership was stronger—based on strengths!

Be Willing to Live with Incremental Change

Remember, anything that lowers your rent creates more time and energy and joy. Making changes that move you intentionally toward your strengths typically has to be done over time. Sometimes multiple adjustments have to be made over months or even years. This is often true in the workplace, where you gain credit and greater freedom as you prove more and more what a valuable member of the team you are. The key is to be making progress. In an age of instant gratification, this reality is often a hard one to realize and to accept. But people with a long-term horizon for life change can experience greater contentment with incremental progress.

Summon the Courage to Make the Hard Decisions

People often wistfully imagine a life built around strengths but are unwilling to make the hard decisions to make that happen. Lowering your rent may require sacrifice. You might need to shift work venues, change jobs, change household arrangements, perhaps even change your lifestyle. But what is it worth to you to have peace, to be fulfilled, to know you are becoming more of the person you were created to be? Is a job worth more than that? Is a certain income more important than the life you give up just to make the mortgage payment or drive a nicer car? What trade-offs are you making to have things that really don't satisfy you and might even be preventing you from having a fuller life?

Let me give you an example. A young man I haven't seen in months recently updated me on his life journey. Wesley is a church planter. His strengths lie in his ability to be a ministry catalyst, not a ministry maintainer. In other words, he likes to start stuff but not feed it. The congregation he planted some years ago has done well but has increasingly demanded from him expenditures of time and energy that are more draining than life giving.

> *What trade-offs are you making to have things that really don't satisfy you and might even be preventing you from having a fuller life?*

Wesley made a courageous decision. He pulled his leadership team together and informed them that he could not give adequate leadership to their growing needs. He recognized that a new chapter in the congregation's ministry was going to require a pastor with different strengths than what he has, so he is now helping them find his replacement. In the meantime he is exploring other church-planting opportunities, but he is also considering taking a secular job to make ends meet or even to fund his passion more permanently.

"Reggie," he said, "I believe my ministry should be in line with how God made me. I'm willing for him to give me assignments in line with that." This determination and courage is causing him some necessary discomfort. It is precipitating a move that disrupts cherished relationships. But his long-haul perspective is positioning him for greater personal fulfillment and ministry effectiveness.

Reflection: What rent-reducing strategies will you employ?

Strong Men and Women to the Rescue!

Rich Williams is known as Big Rich in the world of the super strong—I mean physical strength. Big Rich is an icon, a world champion in the competition involving hand strength. Ripping phone books in half, rolling up aluminum frying pans like tortillas, or picking up 172-pound dumbbells—that kind of strong. You get the picture.

Big Rich is impressive for lots of other reasons too, like his size: 415 pounds packed onto a 6-foot-3 frame, with 23-inch biceps, 33-inch thighs, and a massive 66-inch chest. And he's impressive for the size of his heart. He turned down a promising NFL career option so he could follow his passion—working with schoolkids. He travels to schools to do strength demonstrations, and when he has their attention (not hard to do), he tells kids about the importance of reading. He works as an in-school suspension supervisor, getting up at 5:30 each morning to do crossing-guard duty, then spending the rest of the school day working with at-risk and struggling students. Acknowledging he could have made one hundred times more money as a professional athlete, he says that he is completely jazzed by what he does. Now that's strength—put to good use.

You don't have to be a strong man like Big Rich. You just need to be a strong man or a strong woman like you—put to good use.

A better community is waiting on you to take your best shot!

7

YOU HAVE
A LOT TO
(UN)LEARN

"He died at thirty; we buried him at sixty," Mark Twain once purportedly commented on the death of an acquaintance. The walking dead are the people who have quit learning.

If you want to maintain a vibrant life, you are going to be engaged in lifelong, continuous learning. That requires a commitment on your part. Deciding to do anything less will script a life that stays unfinished, whose remaining chapters fail to develop the plotline—a life that falls into a rut or drifts aimlessly. If this sounds too dramatic, then I've struck the right tone. This is serious!

But here's a little secret that we sometimes don't understand: lifelong learning requires lifelong *unlearning*. That's where our discussion begins.

The Unlearning Curve

The unlearning curve often proves as steep as or even steeper than the learning curve. This unlearning may need to occur in various areas of our lives. We may have to unlearn attitudes as well as actions, reactions as well as habits, that guide our responses to others. The unlearning has to take place to clear the decks for the learning that needs to happen. This is exactly what happened with the philanthropist woman at the end of chapter 5, and with the young father in chapter 2 whose view of his neighbor shifted once he knew his story of abuse and neglect. In the first instance, the unlearning was in seeing that instead of changing others by helping them, we ourselves are changed. In the second case, the unlearning was in seeing the loud, drug-dealing neighbor as a person rather than a problem.

But we don't have the room or capacity for new attitudes, new behaviors, or new habits until we first lose the old ones. I am challenging us all to unlearn our sluggish response or lack of action on behalf of our neighbors—people in need, as Jesus would define them. Our communities are counting on us to unlearn—quick!

> We don't have the room or capacity for new attitudes, new behaviors, or new habits until we first lose the old ones.

The way we see others is not the only story line that we may need to revisit. I am particularly convinced that many of us need to unlearn the narrative of our life that is guiding our actions and life contributions. We all have a script in our heads that provides us the big story line for our lives. Maybe it's "Me against the world" or "I've got to show my parents that I'm not a failure" or "Things always come hard for me." Or maybe it's "I am going to make a difference" or "I can help the world be a better place" or "I have what it takes to succeed." These various narratives are highly personal and have been shaped by a lot of things—from our life experiences to our dreams.

I have found that people who are quick to get off their donkeys and help other people have story lines that have room for other people in them. They are not so self-absorbed that they can't respond to the needs of those around them. Typically their narratives allow for a better world—a hopeful theme that somehow they can make a difference in the world.

As part of a volunteer recruitment effort, I interviewed the principal of a Title 1 elementary school in one of our largest cities in front of a bunch of potential workers and contributors. This school has about eight hundred students, with more than four hundred of them non-English speakers. Many of these kids live in poverty or near-poverty conditions. Their parents are not American-born for the most part, so they are reluctant to get involved with the school system or unable to communicate well enough to be partners in educating their child. This means the principal is running the school without the traditional parental support networks that schools typically have in place. Yet she has the responsibility to equip these children with reading skills and other competencies to give them at least a fighting chance to succeed in our culture and in life. This is a lot of responsibility, not to mention a heck of a challenge, for this young school administrator—who is only thirty years old herself!

After the interview, I said privately to the principal, "You are doing amazing work." I meant it. And I wanted to encourage her in her daunting assignment.

Her reply: "You should meet the kids," she said, breaking out in a big smile. "They are so precious!"

That brief exchange provided insight into the internal narrative guiding this wonderful leader. It's not about her—and she wouldn't let me make it about her either. It's about the kids. They are her mission. She is part of an epic mission to give precious kids a better shot at life. This is the story line that she is living out. The challenges she faces pale in comparison to the critical nature of her mission. She is finding ways to get it done, which is why she was spending a Saturday afternoon in a church fellowship hall with people she didn't know but who might be partners in her mission and its success.

If you have the suspicion that your own personal narrative is not big enough to include helping others, you can change it! Please! Unlearn the old plot; write a new one to live by.

You might consider writing your donkey out of the script.

Reflection: What movie, book, or television show best describes your life story?

Unlearning Can Change the World

The unlearning that you are willing to do can change the world.

Take the apostle Paul as a classic example. No one, whether a Jesus-follower or not, can deny that he changed the world through his life and ministry in the first century. In fact, you and I have been significantly impacted by this man whom we probably would not have known unless he had been willing to go through a significant unlearning. It was Paul who gave Christianity its distinctive missionary character. He is the one—not the original twelve disciples of Jesus—who caught the vision for spreading the gospel of Jesus beyond the Jewish culture and homeland to the rest of the world.

Consider how Paul's unlearning changed the world. His writings paved the way for a trinitarian understanding of God. He unlearned his view of God so he could accommodate his encounters and experiences with Jesus and the Holy Spirit. He also unlearned his daily prayer as a Pharisee—"Thank you, God, that I was not born a Gentile, slave, or woman"—to be able to say, "There is neither Jew nor Gentile, neither slave nor free, nor is there male and female, for you are all one in Christ Jesus" (Gal. 3:28). Think of all the implications of that verse—able to be written because a proud religious person was willing to undergo serious reorientation in his worldview and personal prejudices.

> Who knows how your world will change—and your neighbor's world—when you commit to your own unlearning curve?

Who knows how your world will change—and your neighbor's world—when you commit to your own unlearning curve? Identifying the attitudes, behaviors, perspectives, habits, internal narratives, and responses that you want to leave behind is important preparation for the rest of your life journey. The next order of business is figuring out what to put into your backpack.

That brings us to what you need to know.

What You Need to Know

You can frame your learning agenda in four categories that are common to everyone: self-awareness, skill development, resource management, and personal growth. I will give you some items in each category that you might want to investigate. This list is not offered as a complete set of issues that you need to explore. They are mentioned just to get you thinking about your own learning agenda.

Self-Awareness

Unless you know what pulls your chain, punches your buttons, taps into your dreams—whatever—you have little idea of why you do what you do. This certainly has big implications for your interactions with other people, including those you want to help.

Jenn, for instance, tried to please everybody. As a result, she had a real problem saying no to people, even when she didn't want to do what they asked. Jenn worked herself into exhaustion and began to resent people in general, a problematic attitude to have, especially since she worked in a people-helping vocation.

The real reason Jenn was determined to please everyone had nothing to do with their needs. It was all about her need to be liked. Jenn was terrified that if she turned down people's requests, they would not like her. Because her self-esteem was tied up in what other people thought about her, she was unwilling to risk this rejection.

Jenn finally got desperate enough to get help. She went to a counselor who focused initially on Jenn's dependence on other people for her self-worth. They explored where this dynamic came from in her life. Together they discovered that some family-of-origin factors played into creating the inner narrative that controlled Jenn's emotional dependence on others. Next they identified current situations and circumstances that threatened her self-assurance. Jenn began to understand that her self-worth was not on the line each time people made requests of her, especially when the demands were ones she was not willing to meet.

The counselor helped Jenn recognize the unhealthy decisions and actions that pushed her consistently and routinely to violate her own boundaries of emotional and physical health. Jenn had to develop a checklist of conscious thought reversals so as not to fall into the same old emotional catch-22 of saying yes but wanting to say no, then feeling guilty and resentful. She had to stop listening to those old internal mental tapes that kept prompting her to make decisions that kept her in such confusion and misery.

Jenn's life, as you can imagine, got profoundly better as she began to practice better boundary assertion. Rather than feeling helpless against the emotional need to have approval, she was able to develop alternative attitudes and responses that promoted greater psychological, emotional, and physical health. Jenn quit handing her life over to other people. She took control of it. This also meant that when she gave herself to people, they were getting a more helpful, less resentful Jenn. This was the gift of self-awareness.

Self-awareness develops in people who intentionally examine and reexamine themselves. Some areas to explore include the following.

FAMILY OF ORIGIN

As I have talked about already, we all pick up stuff from our families of origin, sometimes good and sometimes not so good. The point of the family-of-origin probe is not so you can decide whom to blame for what. Parents and grandparents can't take ultimate responsibility for your life responses. Those belong to you. But until you know what your family of origin packed into your suitcase, you have no choice but to lug it around.

BOUNDARY ISSUES

Boundaries are the psychological (and sometimes physical) fences in our lives that help us to know where our life territory ends and the rest of the world begins. Maintaining healthy boundaries keeps us from handing our lives over to others, allowing us to retain appropriate control over our own lives. Do you maintain good boundaries or frequently allow other people to run your life? Are you so afraid of hurting other people's feelings that you can't say no to them? Do you

129

feel trapped by their expectations? Are you withdrawn from others, making it hard for them to reach you and to help you, especially when you need their help? Do you wrestle with where your responsibility begins and ends with others?

PROBLEM EMOTIONS

Sometimes at home I approach household duties with a lousy attitude. I pitch in with the laundry or cleaning up the kitchen while muttering under my breath. My wife, sensing my attitude (she's not clairvoyant; I'm just misbehaving in a transparent way), often says she would rather not have my "help" if it is going to come with the price of having to put up with my negative emotional state. She would rather suffer through the extra work without having to put up with my grumpiness.

I'm pretty sure this silly domestic example is instructive for us in our dealings with our neighbors. They know if we are judgmental, critical, hostile, condescending, guilt-ridden, or self-absorbed. You certainly don't want to be telegraphing these or other negative emotional messages to the people around you—especially those who are already hurting enough from their own problems. Instead of lifting their burden, we can actually add to their stress.

YOUR GENERAL OUTLOOK ON LIFE

What is your outlook on life? Do you see the world as a friendly place or a threatening environment? Is it full of opportunities or full of problems? Is it a giant machine to be fueled and operated, or is it a series of relationships to be nurtured and connections to be explored? Do differences (people, places, tastes, perspectives) cause you anxiety or prove intriguing and inviting? Do you think other people's success comes at your expense, or is there room for lots of winners in the world? Is the best yet to come, or is it now behind you? These viewpoints contribute to your disposition toward the world and the people around you.

PERSONALITY

Are you boisterous or quiet? Do you prefer to be around people to energize your spirit, or do you need to retreat from others to recharge your batteries? Are you chipper and upbeat, or do you tend toward melancholy? On and on the questions could go as you probe your personality. Self-aware people have reckoned with their personality. They command it rather than being commanded by it.

PASSIONS, VALUES, AND GIFTS

I have spent nearly a whole chapter on each of these subjects, so we don't need to rehearse them again. Self-aware people know what they bring to the table in terms of their life mission, their core values, and their abilities.

SPIRITUAL CONDITION

Self-aware people have taken stock of themselves spiritually. Some questions you might ponder include the following: What do you think about God? How would you describe your relationship with him? What draws you closer to God? What do the two of you talk about? What is he like? What does he like? What roles do other people play in your spiritual life? How do others know what you believe? How are other people benefited by your faith? How does serving other people play into your faith development?

Loving our neighbors as ourselves demands greater self-awareness while simultaneously gifting us with even more of it! When it comes to helping other people, your self-awareness plays a big role—in your motivations, how you come across to others, and your expectations of them and yourself. At the same time, serving others also helps you

> Loving our neighbors as ourselves demands greater self-awareness while simultaneously gifting us with even more of it!

achieve greater self-awareness—how you react to certain circumstances or people, what biases and prejudices you carry into your dealings with others, and your expectations of yourself.

Reflection: Pick some of the questions asked in this section and respond to those that are the most interesting to you.

Skill Development

A second area for lifelong learning involves developing the skills that you need. These skills run across a wide spectrum—from those we need to gain or keep employment to those we need to pursue our life mission more intentionally.

Here is a sampling of some skill-set categories you might want to consider.

LIFE SKILLS

These are skills that you need in order to accomplish your life tasks. Your own life-situation needs will dictate this learning agenda. Maybe these skills involve knowing how to cook, how to do basic household chores, how to raise kids, how to be a grandparent, how to be a good spouse. Knowing how to develop relationships and nurture friendships also falls into this category. Understanding better how to communicate is a basic life skill that can often be improved. Even knowing how to buy groceries and shop smart for clothes or decorate your home may be skills that you need to work on.

I am wondering how many of us could make our lives so much better simply by improving some of these basic skills.

And as our lives get better, we have more energy and ability to help others.

Job Skills

It is no longer good enough just to continually improve those skills that are called for at work. I live in a part of our country where manufacturing—specifically, textiles—used to be king. In fact, my parents met as workers in a textile plant when they were teenagers. Back then entire towns developed around these industries. My dad grew up in a house in one of those mill villages. The exodus of these jobs to overseas markets in recent decades has left lots of people unemployed, with skill sets that are no longer needed in the current marketplace.

Strategize on how to add skills to your portfolio of abilities. This will make you both more attractive to your existing employer and more employable in the marketplace. You also gain a psychological benefit. Many people feel trapped in their jobs because they have a limited skill set. People who feel trapped do a poorer job than people who don't. This in turn leads to greater job insecurity or job loss. So keep that skill set expanding!

Sign up for online classes. Take advantage of employer-sponsored continuing education. Find someone who will mentor you in technology (maybe your kids!). Not only will your employment opportunities grow, but you will also enjoy a greater peace of mind as a result of knowing that you are more prepared for changing economic conditions.

Serving Skills

We need to know certain things to be good servers. Some years ago I volunteered to help serve at a friend's party. It wasn't long before I realized I wasn't very good at it. I discovered quickly my inability to distribute ice and drinks in a timely manner. We hadn't even gotten to the salads and rolls

133

before I knew I was in trouble. There were problems with my motor skills as well as with my expectations. Not only did I expect compliments for hitting the insides of the glasses with the ice cubes, but I also wanted to join in the dinner guests' conversations, and I became more annoyed by the minute at their lack of attention to me!

> *If you determine you are going to serve your community and your neighbors, why not determine to be good at it?*

In a more serious application, if you determine you are going to serve your community and your neighbors, why not determine to be good at it? That means you probably will have to pick up a few skills. These might be technical or mechanical, like acquiring tutoring skills or basic carpentry skills. But they may also involve attitudinal skills, like how not to be offended at being seen as a servant or how not to inadvertently make people feel undervalued as you serve them.

Reflection: What skills do you need to acquire or improve?

_____

_____

_____

Resource Management

A third arena for our learning is figuring out how we can better manage the resources we have for our lives. Although we have a number of them at hand—like technology or our relationships, for instance—let's focus on the big two: time and money.

TIME

I was once asked by an adviser, "How would you like to spend a year?" The question threw me, but it also revolutionized my approach to scheduling my life. It had not occurred to me that I could determine ahead of time how I would live a year—how many days I would allot to office work, traveling, speaking, writing, leisure, and routine household maintenance. Up to then, I had come up with that information by looking back after the fact at how many invitations I had accepted or appointments I had made. In reality, my former approach allowed other people, not me, to decide how I would spend my days.

Time management also involves knowing how to spend those days. Sometimes we fail to get the most out of a day, because we either squander our time or overload our docket. When I coach people who are struggling with time "deficits," we begin with a time audit of their day in fifteen-minute increments. It becomes easier to adjust how they spend their minutes and hours once they have accurate knowledge of expenditures. This time-audit diary helps my clients see where they lose ten minutes here, a quarter hour there, mindlessly surfing the web or opening YouTube attachments on email blasts or whatever. Pretty soon they see where they are "leaking" time. Patching those holes can add hours back into their days for the things they need to do. Conversely, once they see where they overbudget their time, they can seriously think through reapportioning activities to match real-time availability.

> *Sometimes we fail to get the most out of a day, because we either squander our time or overload our docket.*

Weeks and months need managing too. It is in these time frames that we can get serious about some rhythm to our lives. Some things we want to schedule weekly; other things quarterly or every six months or so. The key is to protect these items in the daily flow. If not protected and planned for there, they won't show up in real life.

Serving other people is going to require that we create some margins in our lives to accommodate the activity. Our service may be weekly or monthly. Whatever it is, we have to figure out how to move it to our daily calendar and protect it. That means reapportioning time currently spent on other things.

Many people combine different kinds of activities to get the most out of their time—like combining business travel with vacationing. This approach works for service projects too. An increasingly employed strategy is to combine leisure travel with mission trips. Families are beginning to tackle service projects on their vacations, either in their communities or overseas. I recently read about a family that took a yearlong mission to five continents and several dozen countries. They had to raise money, plan their service projects, and coordinate with their local contacts all over the world. It was the adventure of a lifetime for them. Most of us can't do what they did, but we can plan one weekend every three months or a week during the summer to serve somewhere together. You don't even have to leave town. Every community has lots of opportunities for this kind of engagement.

The point is that finding time to serve others requires intentionality. Tough choices may have to be made. But the payoff is worth the effort! And the discipline used to figure this out can be applied to other issues as well—like finding time to exercise or spending more time with the people you love or cultivating new friendships.

Remember, how we spend our days (weeks, months, and years) is how we spend our lives.

Money

Managing money involves more than just paying attention to income and expenses. It actually begins with your attitudes *about* money. You probably initially picked these up in your family of origin, where you learned your first lessons about money, including what it represents. How you manage money can be directly affected by these ideas.

My dad was a salesman, living off commission. This meant that his income varied week to week, sometimes significantly. He talked about this openly, especially each Saturday when he found out how much his next paycheck would be. That weekly conversation taught me to worry about money—specifically, to wonder if there would be enough money to make ends meet. This anxiety rarely has anything to do with the realities of my current financial condition. However, it is the script that I learned very early and is deeply laid into my psyche. I routinely have to challenge this old demon of my soul and replace it with another narrative.

Ask yourself some questions to figure out your own attitudes about money. What does money mean to you—prestige, success, power, leverage, access? Do you equate making money with accomplishment? Do you feel like a failure at money? Do you hoard it? Do you love to give it away? Do you medicate your difficult emotions with spending sprees? Is money a drug? Do you compulsively stash it away? How do you make decisions about how to spend your money, and on what? The answers to these questions not only reflect the perspectives that you carry about money; they also control the behaviors associated with it.

When it comes to helping others, not every act of kindness costs money. It might cost more in terms of energy or time or talent than in dollars. In fact, sometimes the easiest thing to do is to write a check!

But helping others very often does involve money. It takes money to fund food banks and run homeless shelters. It takes money to create jobs and provide working capital for micro-economic development.

Americans are the most generous people on earth—if we use charitable giving as a measure. We give about three hundred billion dollars a year to the causes we love—religion, education, the arts, medical research, and so on.[6] Surveys of individual giving reveal that people who make less money actually give a greater percentage of income away than most people who make more. This has to change. Those of us with more need to give more—individually and corporately.

Recently I met a stewardship development professional who helps couples with disposable income figure out how to increase their level of giving. The idea is to make a percentage increase over several years. He's taking couples from 5 percent to 25 percent, and some even to 90 percent. The only thing rising faster than their giving is their joy in making a difference through helping others.

> *Those of us with more need to give more—individually and corporately.*

If your business can fund another job, then do it! If you can sow an income-producing initiative, then do it! If you can hire something out from your house that can help others, then do it! As you can see, I'm not just talking about giveaways here—I'm talking about creating work for people. I'm talking about our being willing to alter our bottom line so others can get off the bottom.

We can sit around and wait on the government or someone else to take initiative. We can hope that CEOs will willingly reduce the criminal disparity between what they make and what their company employees make. We can pray that corporate boards of directors will be smitten with a conscience and a sense of stewardship for our communities. Keep hoping. But do something yourself! Have a community garage sale for charity, create a pool of investors to fund a kid's summer job, sell lemonade—whatever. You get the picture.

YOUR BODY

I should make honorable mention of your physical body when it comes to managing resources. You might not think of your body as a resource to manage, but it is. Things that we do or don't do—like exercising adequately or practicing good nutrition or getting enough sleep—contribute to the energy we have for helping others.

Tackling other people's issues requires emotional stamina. This can be significantly impacted by our physical regimens. I am not suggesting that you have to be the perfect specimen of health to be useful to others. That requirement would leave most of us out! But it just makes sense that increasing our margins of energy and health can make us more available to others.

Reflection: What personal resources do you need to develop or to manage better in order to make a stronger contribution to your community and to people you want to help?

Personal Growth

A fourth category for you to consider as you learn your way forward is the arena of personal development and growth. Ask yourself, *What do I need to learn in order to feel like I'm growing as a person?* Then develop a learning strategy that allows you to be proactive in addressing this need.

For example, this past week I had lunch with a seventy-seven-year-old friend. He is starting a new business and wanted to tell me about it. During our conversation he asked me, "What should I be reading these days?" That kind of

139

commitment to personal development and learning accounts for this man's lifelong success.

The list of items to include in this section is as long and varied as each person reading this book. Many people would put spiritual growth as an important lifelong aim here. Learning more about emotional health would certainly fall in this area. Improving relationship skills might be a need for you. Expanding your knowledge in a particular educational interest—even pursuing additional academic degrees—might be on your learning agenda. Picking up a mechanical skill or carpentry, taking up painting houses or canvases, learning a new technology—the list is as intriguing as your imagination and curiosity.

Learning from Life

A key ability to incorporate into your portfolio of life skills is the capacity to debrief your life. Military planners debrief their missions. Disaster relief teams debrief their responses to various catastrophes in order to be more ready for the next time they will have to respond to emergency situations. NASA engineers and scientists debrief astronauts after each mission to determine how future space ventures can be improved. In each case, the debriefing creates new knowledge and builds learning by uncovering what each person knows. In a sense, before the debriefing occurs, they don't know what they know.

Learning to debrief your own life experiences can help you capture insights and understandings that are then available to you in other life situations. Here are some important questions you can ask yourself as part of your debriefing routine.

- *What did I enjoy about this experience?* The insights here yield important clues not only about your preferences but also about your values and considerations

140

for future decisions. It is simply astounding that many people wake up every day and choose to do things they don't enjoy—at their work, in their leisure, with their relationships, even with their food choices!

- *What did I not enjoy about this experience?* The flip side to the question above also yields important information to help you avoid some repeat situations, or to figure out why you felt or reacted the way you did. Be honest with this evaluation, even if you don't initially like what you discover.

> Learning to debrief your own life experiences can help you capture insights and understandings that are then available to you in other life situations.

- *What worked—and why?* This question may seem obvious, but often people operate under unchecked assumptions about why something was successful. You might inappropriately credit an action or attitude that really had little or nothing to do with some actual outcome, either a success or a failure. Without this exploration, you may fail to uncover the secrets to even greater success. You may also enter other situations with unwarranted expectations.

- *What can apply to other situations?* Many life lessons have application across the board or at least in some other areas of our lives. For instance, learning how to affirm people in the workplace is a skill that can produce positive results at home as well. Developing patience in mountain climbing might also save your life at lower altitudes during an emergency.

- *What did I learn about myself?* Every time you learn something about yourself, you are closer to living an intentional life. What pushed your hot buttons? What happened that caused you anxiety? What triggered your fear response? What gave you the greatest sense of accomplishment in the project?

When we don't know these things, we fail to handle ourselves and situations in ways that help us learn and grow. Learning about yourself enables you to bring about the most significant but hardest change in your universe—changing you!

Using these questions can help you in your quest to offer your best contribution to others. If certain activities or venues make you uncomfortable, you need to know why. The insights might point you in another direction of service or simply relieve your tension in the current assignment.

For example, Maggie didn't know why she was so afraid every time her youth group volunteered to serve food to the homeless in one of the city parks in her community. Since she was one of the adult sponsors, it was her job to make the experience a great one for the teenagers in her group. When she finally talked through her feelings with one of her pastors, she was able to finger the source of her anxiety. As a highly ordered and controlled person, Maggie felt out of her comfort zone in a setting that was unpredictable. Serving the homeless can certainly be that! Maggie was afraid of being inadequate in her conversation with homeless people whose lives seemed so out of control.

Once she realized that the source of her problem was her own insecurity, Maggie was able to relax around the people she was serving. She let go of the expectation that she would be able to "fix" the dilemmas faced by these people. Maggie further understood that her service in providing a hot meal was bringing some stability into their lives. She could concentrate on the gift of the moment and not assume responsibility for situations beyond her control.

Maggie not only found greater joy in her service; she also realized other areas of her life where she had been sensing similar emotional turmoil. She began to apply her learning in those areas. Her relationship with her teenage daughter dramatically improved when Maggie was able to be less controlling.

This is the power of life transformation that can be unleashed when we debrief our experiences as a learning discipline.

Reflection: Using the questions above, debrief a recent experience of helping others, and see what you can learn from it.

Learning Partners and Patrons

Whom we learn from can make all the difference in what we know. Life debriefing is best done with other people you trust—a life coach, counselor, spouse, or friend. The list of learning contributors for any two of us will not look the same. But categories of people for you to consider will certainly include some of the following. Let's take a look at whom you might want to include in your learning journey.

Family

You didn't choose your family of origin. And you didn't choose the early lessons it handed to you. But you *can* choose the ultimate life lessons you want to keep with you. You have lessons you can build on while leaving other ways of thinking and behaving behind.

The attitudes and behaviors that keep tripping you up need to be left behind. Those inner tapes that contain recordings of conversations and criticisms that tear you down need to be erased and recorded over. Those memories of hurtful episodes

143

need to be healed. These actions may require some serious unlearning that involves professional counseling and cognitive therapy to help you identify what needs to change and how you can make those psychological and emotional shifts.

On the other hand, encouraging sentiments you have received through the years need to be fanned into flame. The fires of family affirmation need to be stoked.

The instructors in your family of origin include more than just your parents. Siblings can and often do play a very important role in shaping early life lessons. They can continue to shape life for you as you grow older. In-laws often contribute to your life learning, from providing wisdom to career counseling to emotional support and insight. They may present a challenge as well, especially if your spouse has been wounded by them in a significant way.

Mentors, Coaches, and Counselors

Sometimes we need to import insight into our lives from people whose special knowledge can accelerate our learning—mentors, coaches, and counselors.

Who is mentoring you? In what ways? Some mentors afford you the chance to hang out with them for some face-to-face time and heart-to-heart learning. Some of them can't—because they're dead! Yet through print or audio recordings, you can spend any evening with the greatest minds in the history of the planet.

Why not get a coach? A whole new genre of helpers is emerging in the field of life coaching. Some life coaches are therapists who have decided to move beyond pathology-based therapy to a more positive and holistic approach in helping people. Life coaches don't just deal with obstacles; they also deal with opportunities.

And you don't have to limit the coaches in your life to paid professionals. Colleagues and acquaintances who aren't afraid to ask you the hard questions, who can create tension in your thinking in order to inspire creative thought—these people perform a coaching role.

If you need the help of a gifted counselor, get it! These people come in very handy in dealing with difficult emotions and difficult people. Maybe the most difficult person you deal with is you! Counselors are especially good at helping you find the source of "stinkin' thinkin'" and rescripting those internal conversations that keep you wed to unhealthy and unproductive attitudes and behaviors.

Friends

"Reggie, you know you are going to have to forgive Bobby."

This advice came from a friend at a time of great personal and professional challenge for me. A trusted co-worker had betrayed me and thrown our organization into enormous conflict. I was not yet ready to do what my friend advised, but his concern for me—that I would not be diminished through the experience by poor reactions on my part—has never been forgotten. We all need people who will tell us what we need to hear, not just what we want to hear.

> We all need people who will tell us what we need to hear, not just what we want to hear.

These kinds of friends are not developed overnight. You need to be cultivating them right now. There will come a time when you need them! They are essential players on your lifelong learning team.

Peers

Not everyone can be (or should be) your best friend. You need people who round out your life perspective. Peers can include friends as well as co-workers or people you live with. You need to choose carefully here—the company you keep will determine your capacity for growth.

Candidates for this role usually share some key affinities with you. They may face similar life situations (such as newlyweds or empty-nesters), share similar work assignments, enjoy the same hobby, or even be engaged in similar personal development challenges (such as weight loss or spiritual formation). I think we pay too little attention to these casual relationships when it comes to what we can learn from the people involved.

Professionals and Occupational Advisers

You need people who can contribute to your vocational aptitudes. Their contributions might range from helping you get inside the door of an industry to helping you move up the ladder to a new position. These life learning partners also contribute in other areas where you need help—like financial experts for investment planning or personal trainers for physical fitness or pastors for spiritual development.

This category also includes people who can bring you up to speed in an area of your life mission or your passion for helping others. For instance, if you have a heart to help teenagers, maybe a high school guidance counselor could add a lot of insight. You might want to talk with a sociologist or community organizer to help you figure out how to mobilize people for community improvement. When you get off your donkey, it really helps if you know how to do what you want to do!

People You Serve

"We have a partnership," Amy told me as I talked with her about her ministry in an inner-city area. Amy coordinates the efforts of several hundred people each week in multiple community-development projects. "We have homeless people who serve other homeless people," she said. "Everyone contributes. We can all learn something from each other."

> *The people we help can be great learning partners, especially if we listen! They can broaden our perspectives, challenge our assumptions, and help us in our own self-discovery.*

The people we help can be great learning partners, especially if we listen! They can broaden our perspectives, challenge our assumptions, and help us in our own self-discovery. They are great gifts to our lives.

Reflection: Who do you need to learn from? How will you learn from them?

Back to School!

Even school has a role in lifelong learning for some of us. Nancy had begun working with her congregation's clothes closet ministry, which was located in a declining part of town. Her desire to serve the poor quickly grew as she became more involved in meeting their needs. Nancy began a degree program in social work, and when her church relocated, she stayed in the old location as the director of the community center that had been launched there. Maybe, like Nancy, your lifelong learning will lead you right back to school.

When you decide to get off your donkey, you make a decision to be helpful. This requires that you be a learner. What do you need to learn? How will you learn it? Who will you learn from? These questions frame your lifelong learning agenda. Pursuing them will help you grow personally. And you will make some other people glad you did!

8

KEEP SCORE—
MAKE IT COUNT!

I have yet to hear anyone say to me, "I am hoping to waste my life, and I want to get started as soon as possible." Nor have I heard, "I have no desire to make a difference with my life." What I *have* heard over and over is some rendition of a common theme: "I want my life to count!"

Everyone has some dreams and ambitions. But having dreams and ambitions doesn't make you special. What separates some people from the rest of the pack is their ability to translate their aspirations into specific accomplishments and concrete results. These people don't just hope that their lives count; they are making sure they do—by keeping score!

Identifying your life mission, figuring out your core values, assessing your strengths, and developing a learning path—then applying these insights in helping others—are all keys to making a difference in the world and to enjoying an abundant life. In this final chapter, I'll share with you my firm conviction that you will accelerate both your contribution to others and your own personal development if you keep score. By that I mean being able to articulate the actions you want to take and keeping track of how well you are doing them. This helps you pay attention to the results you get. I am urging you to be ruthless with yourself when it comes to this life practice. After all, if you lose, we all lose.

Epic Wins

Game developers for video game and internet users create what they call "epic wins" as part of their architecture. This win always includes some kind of score—whether it is amassing points, taking out bad guys, battling aliens, or making progress on some declared goal. Keeping score is the key to motivating players to get engaged with and stay engaged with the game.

> When human beings are able to identify objectives and chart their efforts, they achieve remarkable things.

The same is true in real life. When human beings are able to identify objectives and chart their efforts, they achieve remarkable things—whether it is breaking the four-minute mile or putting a man on the moon.

I see the same dynamic at play in organizations that want to better their communities. Most of my work is with faith-based groups, helping them engage and bless their cities and neighbors. Here are just a few of the epic wins that some of these organizations have determined to achieve:

- eliminate illiteracy in their school district
- raise the high school graduation rate to 90 percent
- reduce the crime rate in crime-ridden multihousing projects

- collect one million pounds of food for the local food bank
- integrate a community of refugees into American culture
- create an after-school program center for every Title 1 school in their district (forty-one of them!)

The leaders and people who are engaged in these efforts are not just chasing an illusory wish. They are creating scorecards to help them chart and celebrate their progress. These teams wrestle with what to measure to ensure their success. They are building coalitions of players across all domains of their cities (government, business, education, and so on), along with raising money and training hundreds and sometimes thousands of volunteers.

The commitment of these organizations to keep score is paying off. Last year I was able to speak at a volunteer appreciation banquet for one of these community efforts. Their backpack program sends food home with food-challenged kids over the weekend. Hunger is a leading cause of diminished learning potential, contributing to illiteracy. By attacking hunger, this organization aims to increase the literacy rate substantially and to give students a better chance at succeeding not just at school but in life as well. Up to a thousand backpacks are packed with six thousand pounds of food each week—all in pursuit of *zero*. That's the number of hungry kids they are shooting for in their school system.

What are their results so far? Over three hundred volunteers gathered in that small town to celebrate the epic wins of higher test scores, higher attendance, and fewer trips to the school nurse—on every campus where their backpack program is up and running. These numbers reflect real people enjoying better lives.

What is true for organizations is true for individuals as well. The same dynamic comes into play: what gets rewarded

151

(celebrated, counted) gets done. What we pay attention to—keep score on—focuses our efforts and motivates us to achieve epic wins in our lives. In fact, every organization quest I have just mentioned was framed by a person or persons who recalibrated their life mission to make a specific and significant contribution to their communities. Committing to a scorecard to gauge their effectiveness has fueled their passion to help people.

> **What gets rewarded (celebrated, counted) gets done.**

So, if you want your life to be a blessing to others, make a point of tracking whether or not you *are* being a blessing to others!

Reflection: What epic win in serving others are you willing to declare and pursue?

_____

_____

_____

Some Coaching Tips

Let me offer a couple of important coaching tips as you think about developing your life contribution scorecard.

Make Sure Your Scorecard Reflects Your Mission and Life Values

You want your scorecard to fit the life game you are playing. How silly it would be to try to score a tennis match using a golf scorecard. You would have no idea how you were doing and would be certain of only one thing—you're confused! Be careful, then, that the results you are after fall in line with your life mission and with the values that are really important to you.

Too many people are using a life scorecard handed to them by others or by our culture. Making money, being successful, having more stuff, achieving the American dream—these "winning scores" may have nothing to do with what you are trying to accomplish with your life. Build your own scorecard to reflect what is important to you.

Let's say your life mission includes investing in and improving the lives of young people. That ambition carries implications for developing a scorecard that will support this dream. You would probably identify some specific contribution you want to make—something deliverable like mentoring, coaching, spiritual guidance, or career counseling. You might want to determine some key measures of your effectiveness, like better grades, college graduation, employment, or areas of personal development—whatever is appropriate to the contribution you want to make. You also might identify some key strategies or platforms you could explore that would put you in touch with the kids you want to help. This could be sports, business, education, entertainment, a youth group in a faith community, or a particular organization. Finally, you would want your scorecard to track your various involvements in the lives of these young people, such as mentoring sessions, music lessons, birthday celebrations—again, what makes the most sense of what will support your end game. Areas of personal development, platforms, processes, specific measurables—these are the elements of a good scorecard.

Stan's story is an example of changing a scorecard to match a life mission. For twenty-six years Stan pastored a congregation, successfully accomplishing every single church goal that was part of his church culture's scorecard. His congregation was growing and vibrant with thousands of people in its weekly ministry. It was, in everyone's mind, a huge success. Except for Stan, who grew increasingly miserable with each new level of growth and program development.

On a sabbatical two years ago, Stan had a "come to Jesus" time where he figured out what the real source of his discomfort was. He realized he had stymied his personal values in pursuit of all the church-culture goals for success. Stan had always felt that the church needed to be externally focused in serving the community, but he had allowed all the growth to insulate the congregation with the self-absorbed agenda of its own program.

> **Being** church better is proving to be more energizing than simply **doing** church better.

Stan came off the sabbatical with a renewed determination not just to turn things around but to turn them inside out. In less than eight months, he launched a not-for-profit foundation to focus on improving the lives of the tens of thousands of at-risk kids in the public school system in his church's city. The foundation has launched a sports league along with an after-school program involving a growing cadre of mentors and tutors to help kids with their homework. Stan has also engaged the city symphony and choral societies to begin after-school classes in music. The arts council is in talks to do the same.

If you run into Stan today, he will tell you he is having the time of his life and his best years as a pastor. All because he was willing to change his scorecard to reflect his own values and personal mission. And by the way, his church is having its best days as well—living as people of blessing to the community they are a part of. As the church has become more engaged in the community, it has experienced renewal. *Being* church better is proving to be more energizing than simply *doing* church better.

Play to Win; Don't Play Not to Lose

Each of us is in a race for life. What is at stake is much more than an Olympic gold. The world is on the line—and you along with it. It's a race you clearly want to win! If you are a sports observer, you know when a person or team is going for broke or merely playing it safe. That same choice faces us all when it comes to how we approach life. Many people play it safe—so safe, in fact, that they never make or leave a mark.

But not Deborah! "I've made a decision," she told her missional community. Recent changes at work had given her a much higher level of responsibility. When her boss retired, Deborah had been named as interim director of a state government agency. She explained her decision to her friends: "Instead of just keeping things together, I'm going to use this position of influence to get some things done that I think need doing."

Deborah's job involves research and funding for public education initiatives. As a missional follower of Jesus, she has long felt that her daily work in serving the educational needs of her state is her life mission. But she has also felt stifled in the past from being able to offer her best thoughts and work in her office. This interim arrangement with added responsibility and influence has awakened in her a new intensity to pursue her life mission. People around her see a new zest in Deborah's attitude, fueled by her decision to make the most difference she can.

"What's the worst thing that can happen to me?" she joked to her group. "They fire me? I don't want the job long-term anyway. I can't lose!"

Truth is, Deborah *can* lose, and thousands of schoolkids right along with her—if she plays not to win. But thankfully she *is* playing to win, and she's making a way for others to be better positioned in their lives.

155

Reflection: How will you incorporate these coaching tips into your scorecard?

_____

_____

_____

Dealing with Objections

I've had enough conversations with people about their lives to know what some of you are thinking right now. Some of you are experiencing mild discomfort to severe pushback to this whole idea of scorecarding your life. Let me offer some things for you to consider if any of these thoughts are swirling around in your head.

"I don't like the idea of scorecarding." Maybe you are not the sports type, so this metaphor doesn't tap into your motivations. You might need to come up with some other metaphor that works for you. Maybe a key motivational idea for you is to celebrate. What will you celebrate in your life that puts you further down the road toward what you want to accomplish? Remember: what gets rewarded gets done. Celebrating the right things will get the results you are after.

"What if I get the scorecard wrong? I would be doomed!" Okay, so maybe I added the second sentence just for dramatic effect, but I do indeed understand the first one and the anxiety behind it. My answer? Of course you will get it wrong! This goes with the territory, because you are on a learning journey (remember the previous chapter). Things change, you get better at understanding situations, your vision gains greater clarity when you focus on an area—life is fluid! You will make adjustments to your scorecard as all these things play out. But you still need a baseline of intentionality for what

156

you hope to accomplish. If you don't, you will not be able to figure out how you can manage future challenges and changes in a way that keeps you from being knocked off your game.

"It's too late." Maybe for some things, but not for others! Start where you can. There is some contribution you still have time to make. But don't sit around. Get going.

"I don't have time for this." Actually, you don't have time *not* to keep score. People living with no target are guaranteed to hit it. Days, weeks, even months and years can be frittered away with no clear direction. Lost time equals lost living. You won't—you can't—achieve your life results all in the next week, month, or even year or five years. But you might as well begin to live the life you want, helping other people along the way get the life they want.

Enough of these objections. Let's get on with keeping score!

Break It Down

The best way to go about this whole scoring effort is to break it down into manageable components. The first big part is to pick an *arena* of your life—family, work, school, friends, spirituality, finances, health, recreation, community service. Since we're talking about serving other people throughout this book, let's use that arena as an example. You'll want to develop a scorecard that supports your efforts there.

Next, list an *activity* you want to be involved in. This may be an activity that has caught your attention because of a particular need in your community. Ideally, it is something that also lines up with your life mission, reflects your core values, and uses your strengths. Let's say you pick "tutoring elementary school kids in reading." Good choice, since their reading level will determine every other part of their life experiences.

157

The next piece is to think through the *agenda* for your service. You might need some help here. Where will you do this? Who should you talk to at the school? When will you do the tutoring? What kind of training do you need? Be a consultant for yourself. Frame the questions you need answers for in order to proceed.

The next step is to nail the first two *actions* you will take. Your two action items might look like this:

- visit the district or school website to investigate any existing tutoring opportunities
- set up an appointment with the appropriate person at the school

Finally, establish some *accountability*. This step usually involves figuring out whom you are going to empower to keep asking you about this project and its progress. Good accountability also includes a "by when?" component. So assign yourself a due date for each action. Will you get it done this week? Over the next two weeks? Until you have assigned accountability (whom you'll report to and by when you'll do this plan), your action step is still only an idea or a wish.

So here's a breakdown of what the process could look like for someone who wants to begin tutoring:

Arena—community service

Activity—tutoring elementary school kids in reading

Agenda—at Rains Elementary two afternoons a week for one hour

Actions—meet with the guidance counselor at the school; block my calendar

Accountability—report to my best friend; start next week

158

This is not so bad after all! And you can do this kind of scorecarding for any area of your life. For instance:

Arena—marriage enrichment

Activity—weekend getaway

Agenda—conversation about life mission; hiking and relaxation

Actions—calendar the retreat; book a place conducive to relaxed conversation

Accountability—bring my spouse on board with the planning

Or:

Arena—spiritual development

Activity—practice the presence of God

Agenda—create God-sightings diary

Actions—buy a journal; begin praying daily, "Lord, help me see you!"

Accountability—report to my small group leader; begin this Friday

Reflection: Take a stab at developing a scorecard. I've taken the liberty of selecting the arena.

Arena—serving others _____

Activity—_____

_____

Agenda—_____

_____

Actions—_____

_____

Accountability—_____

_____

The Point

By now you've figured out that making your life count is not just about the final score. It's about *keeping* score—being more intentional to make sure the things you want to see in your life actually show up there. Keeping score performs the same function as a mile marker on the interstate—it helps you know where you are and what direction you are moving.

> Making the move from hoping some things happen in your life to practicing greater intentionality can reduce a lot of stress. . . . Advancing through a set of achievable actions is liberating.

Making the move from hoping some things happen in your life to practicing greater intentionality can reduce a lot of stress. Dragging around a ton of "shoulds" with you all the time gets really wearisome ("I should do . . ." or "I should be doing . . ."). On the other hand, advancing through a set of achievable actions is liberating. Once you get in the habit of keeping score, you will enjoy the benefits of feeling that you are making progress.

What I'm hoping in writing this book is to persuade you to add an epic win to your life pursuits, specifically in the arena of serving others. Deciding that you want to contribute to your neighbors and *what* you want to contribute will increase and accelerate what is possible for you to accomplish. Your tutoring of one child might begin a movement of improvement for a whole class or school. Your neighborhood hunger drive might make possible the elimination of food challenges for a family. Your engagement with the homeless shelter may eventually reduce the shelter population count in your city.

There is one epic win that I know for sure will emerge as you serve better your life will be more fulfilling. Make that two epic wins: someone else's life will be better too.

So make life count. Keep score. You are worth it. And so are they!

CONCLUSION

An old story about heaven and hell goes like this. In both places people are seated at a scrumptious banquet. But there's a problem. Every person has long paddles attached rigidly to their arms, making it impossible to bend their elbows so they can get to the food on their plate.

In hell the food is strewn everywhere as people try somehow to shovel it into their mouths. The air is filled with the shrieks and moans of frustration.

Heaven is a very different scene. Laughter and lively conversation create a party atmosphere as people enjoy their food. That's because each person is feeding their neighbor across the table.

You are going to decide whether your community, our country, and our world slides into hell or cranks up the party music. The outcome, I believe, hinges on your willingness to serve your neighbor. We certainly have systems that are broken and need fixing. And I understand and agree with the argument that these broken systems keep a lot of good things from happening. But we can't wait on fixing them to move forward. Besides, I don't know what we can do about them. But I do know that you can make life better in your community, on your street, next door, across the table—wherever your neighbor is in need. There couldn't be a better time for you *and* your neighbor to get some help.

I wrote this book to inspire and equip you to do something to help somebody. Turns out that the somebody who may be helped the most is you! I believe that your becoming a better *you* is the key to success for yourself and everyone around you. We all need your best self to show up. This is why becoming more intentional with your life is so important. We need you to discover more completely your life mission and understand the values that motivate you. We need you to bring your best game—your talents and your abilities. We need you to ramp up your learning so you can grow into your future. And we need you to develop a scorecard that supports the contribution you want to make.

> There couldn't be a better time for you *and* your neighbor to get some help.

Fortunately, all these things your neighbor needs from you are items you want for yourself as well. By helping your neighbor, the return gift is that you are helped in becoming the person you want to be. And as you become more of that person, your capacity to be a help to your neighbor increases. It's a beautiful win-win. Wouldn't it be just like God to design a world where the best thing you can do for yourself is to help someone else?

So here are a few last words that I hope will get you moving off that donkey of yours.

Get your act together! Think through all we've talked about. Fill in these blanks as much as you can.

I would like to help _____

by doing _____

_____ (your mission).

The most important reasons I want to do this are _____

_____

_____ (your values).

I have the following skills and abilities to work with:_____

_____

_____ (your strengths).

To move forward, I need to know _____

_____

_____ (your learning).

I will know I am winning at this when _____

_____

_____ (your scorecard).

Go first! Don't wait on someone else to take the lead. Whatever you want to see happen, start doing it. Call the school. Drop some clothes off at the homeless shelter. Visit the food bank. Take some soup and bread down the street. Hire somebody. Register with the Salvation Army or Habitat for Humanity for their next project. Do something! Now!

Call a party! Don't be stingy and hoard all the good for yourself. Be a viral agent—spread the action around. Get others on board with

> *Don't wait on someone else to take the lead. Whatever you want to see happen, start doing it.*

you. Get your neighborhood book club involved. Recruit your Sunday school class or church small group. Sign up your golf buddies—*then* ask them. Line up your co-workers at the office. This doesn't have to be a forever commitment. The point is to get some synergy with others for your project. You just want to get something going. And you will have gotten some more people off their donkeys. You'll be doing them—and your community—a favor.

My dream is that you and I and millions of others will change our country. That city by city, neighborhood by neighborhood, we will unleash a tide of good that will raise all ships. That we will rebuild the fabric of our communities so people can have a shot at a better life. That the confidence in ourselves as a country will be restored. That we will rewrite the narrative of impending doom and gloom into a song of joy. That God's people will call the party and lead the way.

It's not utopia I'm hoping for.

It's the kingdom come.

NOTES

1. 2012 Giving USA: "The Annual Report on Philanthropy for the Year 2011" (Bloomington, IN: Indiana University, 2012).

2. Tom Rath and James K. Harter, *Wellbeing: The Five Essential Elements* (New York: Gallup Press, 2010).

3. "Giving and Your Community Wellbeing," *Gallup Management Journal*, November 30, 2010, 1.

4. Ibid.

5. *Chariots of Fire*, directed by Hugh Hudson, 1981.

6. 2012 Giving USA: "The Annual Report."

Dr. Reggie McNeal enjoys helping people, leaders, and Christian organizations pursue more intentional lives. He currently serves as the missional leadership specialist for Leadership Network of Dallas, Texas.

Reggie's past experience involves over a decade as a denominational executive and leadership development coach. He also served in local congregational leadership for over twenty years, including being the founding pastor of a new church. Reggie has lectured or taught as adjunct faculty for multiple seminaries, including Fuller Theological Seminary, Southwestern Baptist Theological Seminary, Golden Gate Baptist Theological Seminary, Trinity Evangelical Divinity School, Columbia International Seminary, and Seminary of the Southwest. In addition, he has served as a consultant to local church, denominational, and parachurch leadership teams, and has been a seminar developer and presenter for thousands of church leaders across North America. He has resourced the Office of the Army Chief of Chaplains (the Pentagon), the Chaplains' Training School (Fort Jackson), Air Force chaplains, and the Air Force Education and Training Command. Reggie's work also extends to the business sector, including The Gallup Organization.

He has contributed to numerous publications and church leadership journals. His books include *Revolution in Leadership*, *A Work of Heart*, *The Present Future*, *Practicing Greatness*, *Get a Life!*, *Missional Renaissance*, and *Missional Communities*.

Reggie has a BA from the University of South Carolina, as well as an MDiv and a PhD from Southwestern Baptist Theological Seminary. He and his wife, Cathy, make their home in Columbia, South Carolina.

Now that you've decided to
GET OFF YOUR DONKEY,
What's Next ?!

Whether you are a community leader or a small group leader, or it's just you, go to **www.getoffyourdonkey.com** for more resources and ideas!

You'll find:

- small group discussion starters
- videos
- ways to share and learn what others are starting
- church campaign materials
- and much more!

Reggie is also on Facebook:
www.facebook.com/ReggieMcNeal